NO
LANDING
PLACE

Volume 2

Edward Doylerush

Midland Publishing Limited

Contents

First Published in 1999 by
Midland Publishing Limited
24 The Hollow, Earl Shilton, Leicester
LE9 7NA, England.

ISBN 1 85780 090 7

Printed in England by
Ian Allan Printing Limited
Riverdene Business Park
Hersham, Surrey, KT12 4RG

Midland Publishing Limited
is an imprint of Ian Allan Publishing Limited

Front cover photograph: Wreckage of B-17
Fortress 44-8639 of 351st Bomb Group, US 8th
Air Force, which crashed high on Craig Cwm
Llwyd on 8th June 1945 with the loss of 20
airmen. *Russell Zorn via Ian McLachlan*

DEDICATION

This work is dedicated to the memory of all
Royal Air Force, Commonwealth, and Allied
airmen, Air Transport Auxiliary pilots, and Air
Training Corps cadets who lost their lives on
and around the mountains of Snowdonia.

Foreword

by

Don Charlwood

Today, in the year 1999, the youngest aircrew who trained over the Welsh mountains during the Second World War are aged about seventy; the older ones among us have passed eighty. How good it is for all of us veterans to have Edward Doylerush's vivid and detailed records of some of our less fortunate fellows.

He has not only recorded the circumstances of their accidents but has reached their crash sites on foot – places he regards with fitting reverence. He has also traced numerous survivors and next-of-kin, always guided by his belief that researchers in this field are guardians of sacrifices that future generations might otherwise not know. He has gone beyond the war years to later accidents, to the era of the Vampire, Canberra and Meteor.

As an embryo navigator I first looked down on Snowdonia in 1942 from the Ansons and Wellingtons 1Cs of RAF Training Command. Lacking radar, we had been warned to stay at least a thousand feet above the height of Mount Snowdon unless we could see where we were. In fine weather this was easy enough; indeed in fine weather I became entranced by the scenery of North Wales and resolved to get to know it on foot – always providing I survived Bomber Command. But caught in poor weather I soon realised I had first to survive training over this formidable terrain.

Particularly daunting were some of our night exercises. Anxious exchanges between crew members were commonplace. It must be remembered that we often came from different countries; were only just getting to know each other, to measure each other's capabilities.

The bomb-aimer was the navigator's eyes. Our particular bomb-aimer was a London optician; I was a farmhand from an Australian sheep property; our skipper was a terse Western Australian. How anxiously I used to wait on the bomb-aimer's pinpoint! As we groped in murk from Lichfield to the Irish Sea, how frequent were our differences of opinion as to just where we were!

Bomb-aimer: 'Navigator, we are coming up to the coast near the mouth of the Conway . . .'

Pilot (interrupting): 'That doesn't look like the sea ahead of us!'

Bomb-aimer: 'I reckon that's the Great Orme's Head off the port bow – now I've lost it! The cloud has come over again.'

What now? If I go forward for a look I'll do no better – worse, in fact, since my vision is impaired from working under a light.

How many times alarmed exchanges must have preceded fatal accidents – words we will never know, except for those remnants that survivors have passed to Eddie Doylerush, remnants spoken in American, Canadian, Australian and other accents, spoken also in German. Sometimes the Welsh mountains and their weather reduced friends and enemies to equal impotence.

How interested I have been to read in these pages of two fellow Australians' pursuit of a Heinkel, which they shot down near Gwalchmai. The skipper of the Beaufighter involved was Mervyn Shipard whom I was shortly to meet after the war as an airline pilot when I was in civil air traffic control. Eventually he flew for years with Qantas.

Happily my main association with North Wales was recreational. Having been so impressed by its precipitous hills and valleys from the air, I sought it out on foot in the summer of 1943, soon after finishing a tour of operations on Lancasters. Each day I set out on long walks from Tal-y-Cafn, in the Conway valley, always advising the redoubtable PC William Jones of my intentions. He had already gained a fine reputation for mountain rescues and didn't altogether approve of the fact that I was walking alone. He relented when I told him that my intended companion had been lost with the Pathfinders soon after he and I had made our bookings. He so much wanted to join aircrew himself, but couldn't be spared.

It was on my last and longest walk that I came across the twin lakes, Llyn Dulyn and Melynllyn. I didn't know then that I was in an area of many fatal crashes, but I felt the place malevolent, especially around Llyn Dulyn with its dark surface and overhanging precipice. In 1989 my son camped there overnight; he too found it eerie, a place conducive to such reports of apparitions as have been related to Eddie Doylerush. Nearby I came across the remains of what proved to be Ken Archer's Anson, a find that later led the writer of this book to me and eventually led me to Ken Archer himself in New Zealand.

Again and again I have been drawn back from Australia to Snowdonia, the last time in 1995 when my wife and I once more enjoyed the hospitality of Eddie and Mary Doylerush at Roe Wen. We readers have much for which to be thankful to him, not only for the meticulous detail he is able to pass to us, but for the great readability of his text and the compassion he brings to these tales. It is a privilege to be asked to write a Foreword to such a book.

Don Charlwood,
Templestowe, Victoria   January 1999

Don Charlwood looking for an escape route from the dark waters of Llyn Dulyn, the heart of crash country, in 1978.
Ron Waldron

Preface and Acknowledgements

In this, my fourth book on aviation history in Wales, I feel some explanation is due to readers on the origins of my interest in the subject. In the long dry summer of 1977 the local mountains of the Carneddau Range beckoned and I started climbing ever higher onto them. On one of these forays I came across the wreckage of an Avro Anson. I was initially concerned when I heard this aircraft fly low overhead westwards in cloud in May 1959, and I was able to advise RAF Valley this when a report on the radio that evening indicated that it was missing. It was found high on the western end of the 2,000 feet Tal-y-Fan the next morning. The crew of two and their passenger, a Group Captain, who was being flown to Northern Ireland, had been killed outright when the aircraft was diverted to RAF Valley to make another pick-up.

The Anson that I came across was a type I had flown in as an Air Training Corps cadet in wartime, though a later mark. At that moment I became an aviation researcher and writer quite by accident, and no pun is intended. I was joined at the wreckage by someone else who had known exactly where to find the remains. His name was Alan Moreton, and he gave me a list of fifty crash sites in Snowdonia, compiled by the RAF Valley Mountain Rescue Team. I spent all my spare time that summer and up to the winter snows, and since, trekking up to many of the sites to look at the remains of favourite aircraft such as Mosquitos, Beaufighters, Spitfires, and Halifaxes – the latter a type in which I had my first memorable flight in 1944. As I examined each site I pondered on the fate of the airmen involved, assuming they had all lost their lives. A colleague, Glyn Pritchard, like myself a former pupil at the

ATC Tal-y-Cafn Gliding School, hearing of my interest loaned me a copy of a Blackwoods magazine with an article titled 'A Long Time' by Don Charlwood. As an RAAF navigator, Don came to Wales in 1943 for a spell of summer leave after surviving operations with the Lancasters of 103 Squadron at Elsham Wolds. Returning from Carnedd Llewelyn, he sheltered from a sudden thunderstorm in a remote farmhouse known as Rowlyn Uchaf (Upper Whirlpool). The farmer told him that he was not the first airmen there that year, a New Zealand pilot had staggered in there in January, 17 hours after crashing on Foel Grach in an Anson.

I was instantly amazed that there could be survivors from mountain crashes and became determined to discover from official records if there were any more, a lengthy business. I found that within the area of the Snowdonia National Park and its extension to the mountains of the Lleyn peninsula there had been a hundred upland crashes up to 1960, with many more survivors than I anticipated. Many of them owed their lives to the efforts of the RAF Llandwrog Mountain Rescue Team. I set about trying to trace at least one survivor from each survivable crash, in the UK, Canada, Australia, New Zealand, and the USA. My first success was Ken Archer, the New Zealand pilot I first heard of. The account of his flight and survival was riveting. Other researchers unstintingly gave information and photographs. The result was *No Landing Place,* published in 1985. There was so much subsequent interest and further survivors traced since then that a sequel was inevitable to do justice to those involved. I met Don Charlwood in 1978 when, with my brother-in-law Ron Waldron, we made a memorable hike to Llyn Dulyn to look at the Whitley remains and pay our respects to the memory of the crew, and to guide Don back to Rowlyn Uchaf, a visit he made again in driving rain!

My family moved to Rhos-on-Sea in 1938, but each school holiday my mother whisked my brother and I back to her roots in the Wirral.

So it was at Christmastime 1940, nicely in time for the continuing night Blitz. We spent the evenings and early hours under the stairs and stout tables as bombs rained down on Liverpool docks and on the Cammell Laird shipyards at Birkenhead. Odd aircraft dropped their bombs and land mines far too close at times, shaking plaster from the ceiling. We waited impatiently for the siren to sound the 'All Clear', and for mother to realise that discretion was the better part of valour and retreat to Wales, where we could view the destruction of Merseyside from a safe distance. It was with these events in mind that in 1989 I met two of the Luftwaffe airmen who had contributed to our disturbed nights (Chapter 1). Strangely, when I shook hands with them, I felt no animosity.

While the crash sites themselves are most interesting, with remains of aircraft not even in museums today, it was the human aspect which was so moving. The majority of sites I regard as memorials to those airmen who lost their lives in the cause of freedom. I sincerely hope that the remaining wreckage is left on site so that there is always a marker left for posterity. *Look and Leave !*

Several of those who shared the following stories with me are no longer with us. Not only were they volunteers for aircrew, I shall always remember them as gallant gentlemen and unsung heroes.

Following Peggy, my terrier companion on many of the early walks, along came game little Cindy, a Jack Russell terrier, who accompanied me for research on the hills for the last three books. She died just before publication of this book, her part in aviation history is fulfilled. The high peaks will not seem quite the same now without her by my side.

For the sake of continuity, Welsh place names are generally used as they appeared on maps and official documents of the time.

I must apologise in advance for any inaccuracies in this work and anyone inadvertently left out of the acknowledgements.

Any correspondence will be welcomed by the author, via the publisher please.

Acknowledgements

A special thank you again to Don Charlwood for his moving foreword, and to the following without whose help this work would have been either much slimmer or impossible; Wg Cdr D Forbes, Flt Lt B Cooper and Flt Lt P Rowan of East Lancs Wing ATC; AAIB, Dept of Transport; Air Historical Branch, MoD; Charles and Rowan Birch; Ruby Bishop; Vivien Branscheid, Mark Brittain and colleagues of the *North Wales Weekly News*; Russell Brown; Public Archives of Canada; H G Chubb; Glyn Davies, another ATC ex-pupil pal at 68 EGS, for reproducing many of the photographs; Huw Edwards for pinpointing the site of Vampire VV601; Arthur W Evans; Wg Cdr Brian Hayes, Pathfinder Force Association in Australia; Terry Hill; Michael Bayley Hughes; Scout Commissioner George Hiscocks; Gerallt Jones; Jack Jones; John Glyn Jones; Major C R Kilford CD; Pamela King; Jean Langley; Gp Capt Phil Langrill OBE; *Manchester Evening News*; John Meerwald who once shared Anson flights with me; Wendy Mills, DERA; National Library of Wales; RAF Personnel Management Agency; John Richards for the well remembered climb to Lancaster NE132 remains; Matthew Rimmer for his research on B-17 at Craig Cwm Llwyd; David Roberts; R E (Bob) Roberts; Jill Rutter; David J Smith; D J Thorpe at Bradwell Bay; Hugh Trivett for his Luftwaffe expertise; Glyn Warren; Roger Winlaw; Phil Wren; Judith Wolfe, 'the team' at Midland Publishing, and last but not least, my wife Mary.

Edward Doylerush,
Snowdonia, 1999

Note: If all the aircraft which have crashed in Snowdonia could be erected nose to tail from sea level, they would soar high above Snowdon's summit at 3,560 feet.

Part I

THE
BACKGROUND

Snowdonia: Graveyard of over one hundred aircraft:
Last moments of the Brave.
Summit of Foel Grach with cliffs of Craig Dulyn to the right.

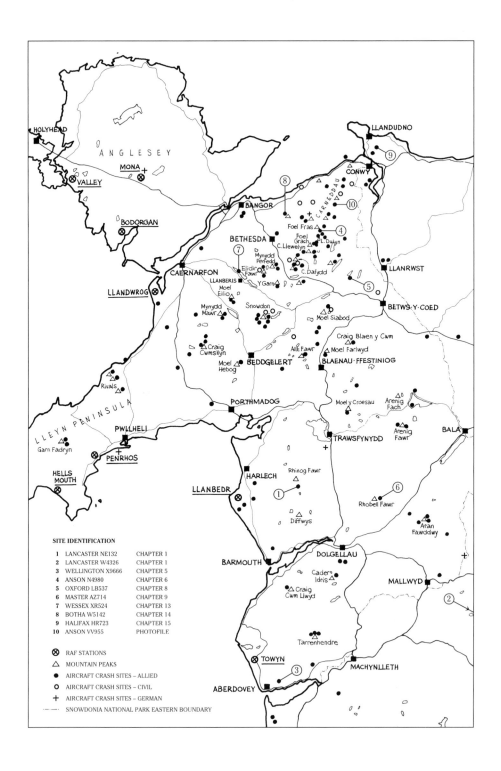

HOLYHEAD

A N G L E S E Y

MONA

VALLEY

BODORGAN

LLANDUDNO

⑨

CONWY

BANGOR

⑧

C A R N E D D A U

Foel Fras △

④

⑩

BETHESDA

Foel Grach △ L. Dulyn

C. Llewelyn △

Mynydd Perfedd △

LLANRWST

Elidir Fawr △

C. Dafydd △

⑦

CAERNARFON

LLANBERIS

Y Garn △

⑤

LLANDWROG

Moel Eilio △

BETWS·Y·COED

Mynydd Mawr △

Snowdon

Moel Siabod △

Craig Cwmsilyn △

Craig Blaen y Cwm △

Allt Fawr △

△ Moel Farlwyd

Moel Hebog △

BEDDGELERT

BLAENAU·FFESTINIOG

Rivals △

PORTHMADOG

Moel y Croesau △

Arenig Fach △

L L E Y N   P E N I N S U L A

PWLLHELI

TRAWSFYNYDD

Arenig Fawr △

BALA

Garn Fadryn △

PENRHOS

HELLS MOUTH

HARLECH

Rhinog Fawr △

①

⑥

LLANBEDR

Rhobell Fawr △

Diffwys △

Aran Fawddwy △

BARMOUTH

DOLGELLAU

MALLWYD

Cader Idris △

②

Craig Cwm Llwyd △

Tarrenhendre △

MACHYNLLETH

TOWYN

③

ABERDOVEY

SITE IDENTIFICATION

1   LANCASTER NE132   CHAPTER 1
2   LANCASTER W4326   CHAPTER 1
3   WELLINGTON X9666   CHAPTER 5
4   ANSON N4980   CHAPTER 6
5   OXFORD LB537   CHAPTER 8
6   MASTER AZ714   CHAPTER 9
7   WESSEX XR524   CHAPTER 13
8   BOTHA W5142   CHAPTER 14
9   HALIFAX HR723   CHAPTER 15
10 ANSON VV955   PHOTOFILE

⊗   RAF STATIONS
△   MOUNTAIN PEAKS
●   AIRCRAFT CRASH SITES – ALLIED
○   AIRCRAFT CRASH SITES – CIVIL
+   AIRCRAFT CRASH SITES – GERMAN
– · –   SNOWDONIA NATIONAL PARK EASTERN BOUNDARY

Chapter One

Update on
No Landing Place

The Last Flight of 'Bachelors Baby'

In 1960, eight year old Peter Green and his family moved from Manchester to Llanfairfechan. He soon made good friends and was introduced by them to the local mountains above his home. Three years later several village lads decided to climb Penmaenmawr mountain in search of fossils and Roman coins. The leader was one Wyn Williams, whose father was foreman at the extensive granite quarry there, and who knew all the routes through this potentially dangerous area.

On this day a thick mist enveloped the mountain summit so they kept close behind Wyn on the stiff climb. Peter Green continues: 'Somewhere around the rocky knoll known as Mynydd Bach our route was to swing sharply to the left, soon taking us to steep cliffs I was not looking forward to meeting. Myself and John Cooper, being the youngest in the party, were about 20 yards behind the others, who were barely visible through the mist. They had passed, and we were level with two men about 20 yards to our right, where the visibility was slightly better. One was seated on a boulder and the other was standing alongside. They appeared to be chatting.

'We lost sight of them momentarily, when one of them shouted after us "Hey Kids!" By now the remainder of our group were out of sight. We turned round and the man standing by the boulder called us over with his arm. As we approached it became clear that they were wearing United States military uniforms, examples of which we had previously seen only at the cinema. The erect individual wore the hat of an officer, very casually. The other, seated, was hatless.

'The officer held up his hand when we got about six yards away, requesting that we come no nearer. The seated man was in his twenties and glanced at us, then cast his gaze downward to the ground. He appeared to be desperately unhappy. The other did not, but had an extremely friendly expression. I asked him were they American pilots. He sort of nodded positively then added "I was the co-pilot." As he said this he pulled a packet of US cigarettes from the breast pocket of his shirt under his unfastened bomber jacket, and tipped a fag out in the only way I had seen Americans do in films.

'The oddness of the pair was now making me feel nervous, if not afraid, though up till now everything about the standing airman was warm and friendly. He smiled a lot. I asked what part of the US he was from. At this, the seated airman looked sharply at his colleague. Both glanced at each other for a few moments and then both looked down at the ground. On a further question, the officer did not answer, but looked at me with an expression of great sadness. When I said goodbye, the officer finally spoke and asked where our friends had gone. I said they were making for the mountain top. "Go after them quickly" he said, "Catch them and tell them not to go to the old quarry today." I had not mentioned the quarry, which was strange. We turned and again I said goodbye. Neither airman replied, but just stared down sadly at the ground.

'We ran like blazes after our mates, and Wyn Williams came down through the mist, followed by the others.'

It was then that Peter Green was told that an American Liberator bomber had crashed in the area during the war, and that since that

9

time young US airmen had been seen by the quarry workers, always in the mist.

Many years later Peter Green read the original volume of *No Landing Place* and discovered the name of the officer he believes he saw – 2nd Lieutenant Art Davis. On being shown a quality photograph of the crew he picked out Sergeant Bill Lorenz as the seated airman. Both men had been killed in the crash of B-24J Liberator 42-99991 on 7th January 1944, along with Staff Sergeant Sammy Offutt, Sergeant Bill Nichols, and passenger Sergeant N Cennemo.

Following the visits of Ace and Lois Shultz, along came two other survivors, Julian and Paula Ertz with daughter Beth, and later Hal and Pat Alexander. Apart from the pleasure of my wife Mary and I being able to show them the glory of Snowdonia, I was able to accompany them to the Liberator memorial and observe the deep feelings that were evident as they recalled the loss of their comrades and their mascot at that lonely place.

Identity tag found in the Liberator wreckage, but this newly recruited US Navy man was not aboard. How did it get there? *Les Jones*

Four of the Liberator's crew at Herington AFB, Kansas, in November 1943. Left to right: Bill Nichols, Sam Offutt, Hal Alexander with Booster, their fox terrier mascot tucked in his flight jacket, and Joe Neiglos. *Hal Alexander*

The remains of Liberator 42-99991 which crashed at Moelfre, above Llanfairfechan, on 7th January 1944. *Robert K Downes ex-USAAF, via W E Griffiths*

There is an abiding mystery left from this incident. In all the luggage and spares strewn across the plateau leading to the crash site, a young local man picked up an identification tag. The details on the tag were those of Roxy R Ambruso, religion, blood type, and month of enlistment – 11/43 . Strangely, quite apart from not being on the Liberator, Ambruso was in the United States Naval Reserve. How on earth did his dog-tag find its way onto a brand new USAAF aircraft?

Enemy at the Door
In 1989 the writer was asked to assist the Welsh independent television company, HTV, with a programme on aircraft crashes in Snowdonia. This was produced for the channel S4C as 'Adar y Ddrycin' (Birds of the Storm) screened on 11th April 1990. For the main story it was decided to make contact with the two German airmen still alive who had survived the crash of the Heinkel He 111 which flew into Llywdmor on 14th April 1941. In late summer the former pilot, Lothar Horras, and wireless operator Kurt Schlender came independently to Wales and were flown separately from Aber (now known as Abergwyngregyn) by helicopter to meet for the first time in 48 years on the mountain where their aircraft had crashed.

Gefreiter Kurt Schlender. *HTV*

Rescuer Ellis Lewis, between Paula and Julian Ertz, at the gate to Blaen Llwyn farm, with National Park warden John Roberts MBE, who set the memorial plaque in place on the crash site. The B-24 first hit the mountain on the skyline above the farm.

Leutnant Lothar Horras. *HTV*

Leutnant Lothar Horras and an eager Gefreiter Josef Brunninghausen in their Heinkel. *HTV*

Following this extraordinary meeting, all the interested parties, including Frau Horras had lunch at the Aber Falls Hotel, during which the writer was able to interview Horras. When I shook hands with him it felt very awkward, then I remembered he had lost fingers from his right hand in the crash, and that he really was our former adversary. Later we drove a little way up the mountain to see Cydcoed, the cottage where Schlender had raised the alarm the morning after the crash. I asked Schlender if we might have a private chat and we wandered off from the rest to sit on a convenient rock near the river. I switched on the tape recorder, but at that moment all the sheep which were browsing around suddenly congregated on us and almost drowned out the recording. Schlender and I exchanged glances and we fell about laughing!

Further information gleaned from these interviews was that in taking off from the short runway at Nantes in western France rockets were used, each giving 400 horsepower for 30 seconds to assist with lifting the heavy bomb load of 1000 Kg armour piercing and one 1,400 Kg bombs. This technique was unique to Kampfgeschwader 28; no other Luftwaffe group used them at the time. After the hot reception at Barrow in Furness trying

to bomb the aircraft carrier HMS *Illustrious*, only the liquid compass remained working. Horras decided to fly back via Anglesey to avoid fighters around the south coast. Soon they became unsure of their position and the pilot eased the controls back to climb. Suddenly Schlender yelled 'Herr Leutnant – mountains!' Somehow they just scraped over 1,750ft Yr Orsedd and dipped into the void beyond. Horras applied full power and the Heinkel was struggling to gain height when it became very dark ahead and they hit the upper slopes of Llwydmor at a height of around 2,200 feet.

Joseph Brunninghausen, who had been with the crew since the beginning, was killed in the ventral (under) turret as it struck the mountain, but the other three survived. Later, in crossing the boulder strewn Afon Anafon, Horras lost his footing, went under,

and came up spitting water to the amusement of Perzonowsky, the observer, who had crossed successfully.

The survivors were eventually moved to Canada, with Perzonowsky being sent to Medicine Hat NCO internment camp No.132. Here, a former doctor of philosophy, Corporal Karl Lehmann, an active communist, was becoming an increasing thorn in the sides of the diehard Nazis there. He translated local papers for the inmates which contained increasingly unpalatable news on the various military campaigns. It was also suspected that he would make a bid for camp leadership. Eventually, either after orders from German High Command came, via a secret radio, to silence him – or Sergeant Major Perzonowsky and three others took it on their own shoulders, or were charged with the task, which they carried out on 11th

September 1944, by hanging Lehmann from a gaspipe in a spare hut. During Lehmann's struggle for life the rope broke the first time.

The RCMP were faced with the unenviable task of identifying the murderers out of 12,000 inmates! Many months later they were found out and came to trial as late as June 1946. In the town of Medicine Hat on the 30th of that month they were all found guilty. At the very moment the death sentence was pronounced by Chief Justice Howson, the school bell nearby started to toll, which sent a shiver down the spines of all in the courtroom, not least the convicted men. The day before the hanging a book was delivered to the jail containing pieces of razor blades. Three of the men tried to cheat the hangman by slashing their wrists, but they were discovered and lived to the next day, the 18th December 1946. All four were hanged at Lethbridge, along with a child killer, this becoming the second largest hanging in Canadian history.

The Bank Holiday Botha

On 23rd August 1942 Blackburn Botha L6318 of No.3 School of General Reconnaissance took off from Squires Gate airfield, near Blackpool. The pilot was Sergeant Herford Linton Pendal who was born in 1910 near Kimberley, South Africa. He had joined the RAF as a pilot officer on a short service commission in 1930, after taking private tuition as one of the first pupils at de Havilland's, Stag Lane, Edgware.

He was badly injured in a low flying crash near Wittering on 24th June 1931 in similar circumstances to Douglas Bader, though without a loss of limbs, and discharged from the RAF in September 1931.

Opposite page: **Fred and Anne Taylor stand by the menacing Swastika on the tail fin of the Heinkel on Llwydmor.** *Anne R Furno*

Oberfeldwebel Bruno Personowsky (centre). *Ifor Hughes*

Photograph on this page:
The reunion of Horras and Schlender in 1989 by the place on Llwydmor where their Heinkel crashed 48 years earlier. *HTV*

Since he later volunteered for the RAFVR he was soon back in the service when war started. Although, like many, he wanted to be a fighter pilot, his role was to help trainee pilots and navigators as a staff pilot at the SGR from where they would be sent to Coastal Command squadrons.

After the sea crossing the Botha flew into cloud just before making landfall on the north Wales coast, though the weather forecast had been for clear conditions. Mrs Morfydd Jones in the farmstead of Cae Defeity above Conway was suddenly startled by the loud roar of a low flying aircraft in the mist. Seconds later it hit a low rocky bank on the north east slope of 2,000 feet Tal-y-Fan near the enclosure of Ffriddlys. Hugh Jones, and his father from the farm rushed through the mist to the scene of the crash only to find the crew of five, sadly, past aid.

15

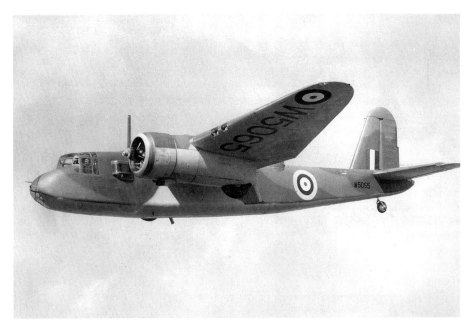

Three of the crew, Sgt R W Patrick, Sgt J B Wood, of the RNZAF and AC1 A Smyth, RAF, are buried at Llanbeblig cemetery, Caernarfon. AC1 Ronald Ibbotson is buried in Colne, Lancashire. His sister recalls that he was a very cheerful person, always singing and laughing with a great gift for music. He played the organ, piano, concertina, piano accordion, ukelele, and Hawiian guitar, and was always willing to help in any project in the community. What a loss.

The pilot, Sergeant Pendal, had breathed his last in the land of his mother, who was born in Builth Wells. Six weeks later his widow bore a daughter, Susan Marie, to bring up on her own.

The deadly cloud vanished later giving a bright Bank Holiday Sunday afternoon, and hundreds of the local populace climbed to the site at 1,500 feet to see the remains of the Botha and debate the loss of five young airmen. Strangely the external pitot head, which detected airspeed for that instrument on the pilot's display, was found with the cover still on. It should have been removed before the flight, and may well have affected the pilot's judgement of airspeed on entering cloud.

Blackburn Botha. *BAe Brough*

Ronald Ibbetson, wireless operator on Botha L6318. *Freda M Stone (niece) via Russell Brown*

Pilot Officer H L Pendal, pilot of Botha L6318 is first right in the group above, and in the open cockpit fighter below. *Both Mrs S M Parashaw (daughter)*

The Rhinog Lancaster

In January 1997, A BBC Wales TV producer asked the writer if I could travel to Harlech and say a few words about a Lancaster which had crashed high on the Rhinog range in wartime. John Richards, a local man, was proposing to place a memorial plaque there near the anniversary of the loss. I was pleased to accept the challenge, since I had not visited this site. It was high time I did. John Richards was our guide.

We started in the valley of the Afon Artro and climbed steadily eastwards. The scenery was different from other parts of Snowdonia with a big bare intimidating rock formation to the north. Between the huffs and puffs of climbing ever higher, I listened while John told us of a great battle that had taken place nearby in ancient times. We followed an old mining track to an abandoned manganese mine. Ahead, an unusually large flock of mountain goats were grazing. Suddenly, not far from the summit ridge of Rhinog Fawr we were amongst many pieces of wreckage. The impact site was higher up against a rock and devoid of vegetation. The TV camera was set up and I said my piece in the rain. I finished with Don Charlwood's words he wrote for a previous foreword, that these airmen had died in a place of great beauty and in a friendly land.

This Lancaster, serial NE132, was on a cross country training flight on 6th February 1945. Flying Control at RAF Llanbedr on the coast noted it flying eastwards. Later its base at 1653 HCU, North Luffenham, Rutland,

reported it missing, coming inland from Cardigan Bay. The crew were seven in number, the pilot and navigator being Australian. Flying Officer David H R Evans was born in Perth, Western Australia and became a dairy farmer. Following his enlistment in the RAAF in October 1942, he gained his pilot's wings in September 1943. He eventually arrived in the UK and came together with his navigator, Flying Officer M W Moon at No 1653 Heavy Conversion Unit. Moon was born in the mining community of Broken Hill, New South Wales, and became a textile salesman until joining the RAAF, also in October 1942. Like many RAAF navigators, his training was in Canada, at the AOS Edmonton.

When the Lancaster was reported overdue Phil Wren of the RAF Regiment at Llanbedr was aroused and asked to arrange a search. It seemed as if it would be searching for needle in a haystack, however he did his duty. 'I headed for the Nissen hut where the guys were sleeping and decided that Lofty was the strongest, so I give him a shake. Nothing happens. I tip him out of bed and kick him hard, which has the desired effect. The ambulance arrives driven by a young WAAF. We get in and drive off. I work out that the route of the plane would take it towards the first high ridge of mountains. We head along narrow lanes towards Cwm Bycham and stop near a shepherd's cottage (Dolwreiddiog). I climbed out and gazed towards those massive heights that I had walked on outings. Suddenly, I saw a small tongue of flame for perhaps two seconds. 'I've got it' I shouted to Lofty, keeping my eyes rivetted to the spot. We aroused the shepherd and asked him to act as guide. We took first-aid supplies and set off, the shepherd in front, Lofty and I, and the game little WAAF in the rear. As we got higher the going got rougher and steeper. Rocks, vegetation, gullies flowing with water, snow and blackness. As dawn broke I was in the lead just below the crest when I spotted an 8 inch length of brilliant red oil feed pipe and burnt pieces of heather and a burnt parachute. The four of us scoured the mountainside and

IN MEMORY OF THE CREW
OF THE LANCASTER WHICH
CRASHED HERE ON THE
6ᵗʰ FEBRUARY 1945

ER COF AM GRIW Y
LANCASTER A FU MEWN
GWRTHDRAWIAD YMA AR Y
6ᵗʰ O CHWEFROR 1945

PILOT/FLYING OFFICER DAVID HENRY ROBERT EVANS. R.A.A.F.
AIR GUNNER Sᵍᵗ ARTHUR DAVID GASH. R.A.F.
FLIGHT ENGINEER Sᵍᵗ GEORGE EDWARD WILLIAM HODGE R.A.F.
NAVIGATOR/FLYING OFFICER MAXWELL WALTER MOON R.A.A.F.
AIR GUNNER Sᵍᵗ HAROLD NIELSEN. R.A.F.
AIR BOMBER Sᵍᵗ CHARLES WILLIAM SOUDEN. R.A.F.
WIRELESS OPERATOR/AIR GUNNER Sᵍᵗ ALFRED ERNEST CLIFF R.A.F.

PAN EWCH ADRE'N OL SONIWCH WRTHYNT AMDANOM
A DWEUD 'ER MWYN EICH YFORY CHI FE ROESOM EIN HEDDIW NI'
TO LIVE IN THE HEARTS OF THOSE
WE LEAVE BEHIND IS NOT TO DIE.

Memorial at the crash site of Lancaster NE132 on Rhinog Fawr. *John Richards*

found enough evidence to identify some of the crew. We descended with Lofty and I doing the carrying. Lower down we came to a dry stone wall. We were too exhausted to climb over so we took it down stone by stone till we could squeeze over. Lofty and I placed our load in the ambulance and collapsed onto the stretchers which our marvellous young WAAF took us back gently to Station Sick Quarters.'

The subsequent investigation showed that the Lancaster had flown into cumulo-nimbus storm cloud and the pilot had lost control. In pulling out of the dive the aircraft broke up with parts breaking off over a wide area. The pilot held on while two of the crew baled out but they were too low. The next morning on the other side of the range, John Richards' aunt, Cathrine Richards found a flying glove on her way to school. Inside were a pair of silk gloves turned inside out.

Flying Officer Moon was buried at Blacon Cemetery, Chester, Sec A Grave 270, along with Sergeant H Neilsen, who was from South America. Sergeants G E W Hodge, A E Cliff, and C W Souden were buried in their home towns. The bodies of Flying Officer Evans and Sergeant A D Gash were never found, so their names are perpetuated on the Runnymede Aircrew Memorial.

Above left: **F/O D H R Evans RAAF, pilot of Lancaster NE132.** *Jocelyn Hughes (sister)*

Above right: **F/O M W Moon RAAF, navigator of Lancaster NE132, on enlistment.** *Wg/Cdr Brian Hayes*

Accident or Sabotage ?
– the Dolwen Hill Lancaster.

A number of Avro Lancasters, for no apparent reason, blew up in the air or dived into the ground without the crews being able to escape to explain the cause. In 1944 at the Vickers-Armstrong Castle Bromwich factory evidence was found of wiring being tampered with; the saboteur was caught.

R F (Bob) Johncock was an air gunner with 101 Special Duties Squadron at Holme-on- Spalding Moor. 'In November 1942 one of the gunners of W4326 reported sick with a cold and asked me if I would take his place for a cross-country exercise over Wales. My own crew was not flying on the 16th so my skipper agreed to me flying with Warrant Officer J Spinney's crew. However, at breakfast on the 15th, the 'sick' gunner informed me that he had been cleared to fly and that I would not be required. I was rather disappointed at the time, but in hindsight, fate had

been kind to me.' Lancaster W4326 took off that night as planned. In the morning not only had it not returned to base, it had not landed at any other airfield.

On the west Wales coast RAF Towyn had been advised that an unidentified aircraft had crashed near Llanerfyl about 0400 hours on the 16th, after an explosion in the air. A mountain search party from Towyn along with police and Home Guard arrived in the area to look for any survivors. At first the wreckage was unrecognisable, being scattered over an area of 3 miles by ½ mile from Llanerfyl to Dolwen Hill. Documents found indicated that the aircraft was Lancaster

The author at the crash site of Lancaster NE132, January 1997. *John Richards*

Flying Officer David Evans (third left) with a 26 OTU Wellington at Wing, Rutland, in mid-1944. There is every likelihood that, with the exception of the instructor on right, the other airmen also became part of the crew of Lancaster NE132. *Jocelyn Hughes (sister)*

W4326 of 101 Squadron. A Lancaster from Holme piloted by Squadron Leader A Reddick took off to assist in the search. It was also believed that another of their machines was missing. After a six hour square search they had to return, for their Lancaster was required for operations. (Although the loss of a second aircraft around this time was suspected by members of 101 Squadron, research has failed to substantiate the claim, which is another mystery).

Eventually six of the crew were found after an extensive search over difficult and lonely terrain, Warrant Officer J Spinney RCAF, Pilot; Sergeant J W Clarke RNZAF, Flight Engineer; Sergeant H W A Collett RNZAF, Navigator; Sergeant A Beach, Air Gunner; Sergeant J Holloway, Air Gunner; and Sergeant C Coleman, Observer. The body of Sergeant J Gould RCAF, Wireless Operator was not found until ten days later.

For the RAF accident investigators this was a difficult case. No other aircraft was involved – only four engines found. It had not struck high ground, but it was determined that an explosion had blown off the complete tail section. Suspicions were aroused then that sabotage may have been the cause. One other factor came into play. As part of the exercise a lake in the vicinity, Bala perhaps, was to be photographed, and so a photoflash from a chute in the rear of the aircraft would have been used. The investigator's report decided that a photoflash went off prematurely in the aircraft, though it could not be said if it went off inadvertently or was deliberately jammed in the chute.

At the time the airfield at Holme-on-Spalding Moor was very accessible and the guard house at the main gate was only a front to log personnel in and out. After that crash, patrols and guard dogs were introduced. A strange coincidence.

Sergeant, later Warrant Officer, J W Spinney RCAF, pilot of Lancaster W4326.
Monica Scribbans (niece) via Charles Birch

Sergeant H W A (Bill) Collett RNZAF, navigator, who survived 15 operational sorties before his loss in Lancaster W4326.
Max Collett (brother)

Completely refurbished engine from Lancaster W4326 crated for delivery to Air Caernarfon Museum. *David Roberts*

Recovery of parts of Lancaster W4326, including an engine by the arm of the JCB, from the wild boggy moor. *David Roberts*

Funeral of Warrant Officer J W Spinney at Towyn cemetery 29th November 1942. *Monica Scribbans (niece)*

B-17 Fortress 42-31321 CC-M of the 569th Bomb Squadron, 390th Bomb Group which, short of fuel, overshot on a forced landing at RAF Towyn. *USAF via David J Smith*

Chapter Two

USAAF Mishaps

THE BOMBERS

Boeing B-17F Fortress 42-3124, of 427th Bomb Squadron, 303rd Bomb Group on 4th August 1943

Walter 'Jud' Johnston was a graduate of Fayette High School, Ohio, in the class of 1935. Even then his ambition was to be an aviator, though he worked first for the Micro-matic Company of Detroit. In June 1942 he joined the USAAF and trained as an air gunner. Sergeant Johnston flew to Molesworth in the UK in April 1943 where he made 25 operational missions over Germany as a rear gunner in B-17s of the 303rd Bomb Group – 'Hell's Angels'. On the late evening of 3rd August 1943 he volunteered to join a crew on a cross country navigational training flight. B-17 Fortress 42-3124 duly took off with eight airmen on board, not the usual ten as on operational flights. Three on board were not the regular crew either. The pilot was 1st Lieutenant James N Pratt from Boise, Idaho.

At 0045 hours on the 4th the Fortress collided with the western side of the unseen 2,800 feet summit of Arenig Fawr a few feet from the top, killing all on board. This mountain stands alone, the only peak for many miles around. It would have been a feat to aim at it in the dark and hit it. The local Home Guard contingent took two hours to climb to the wreck, though there was nothing they could do with exploding .50 inch calibre ammunition. RAF Llanbedr took crash action sending their medical officer. Later in the day Major Hagenbach of the 303rd Bomb Group flew in to Llanbedr and visited the site. Most of the wreckage was removed by 34 MU from Bethesda, and the 2nd Strategic Air Depot from Abbots Ripton.

Sergeant Johnston was only 25 years old, and is buried in the US military cemetery at Madingley, Cambridge. Many years later through local effort, a memorial plaque was erected on the mountain summit. Though later damaged, it was replaced with the aid of a USAF helicopter in 1983. There is a special union between the people of nearby Bala, and Tinley Park, Illinois where 2nd Lieutenant Allan M Boner was from. A resident – Don Konley, who served with the USAF at Burtonwood in the early '50s, has done much to foster this, and has traced some of the crew's relatives. In May 1996 he and the writer were present when a memorial plaque was dedicated on the face of the old town hall at Bala. Local youth and service organisations remember the crew annually with a pilgrimage to the memorial on the summit. Their feeling may be summed up in a moving poem written by a Bala man after visiting the crash site.

The regular crew of B-17 42-3124 'Mr Five by Five', the four officers standing. Identified are 1st Lt. James N Pratt, the pilot, 1st left, 2nd Lt. Allan M Boner, third from left. Bottom row, S/Sgt Walter J Johnson second from right, and T/Sgt Fredric J Royar third from right.
Paul C Royar via Don Konley

Recovery team from 34 MU and civilian helpers on the tailplane of B-17 Fortress 42-3124 on the summit of Arenig Fawr.
Dick Morris, sitting 2nd left

IN MEMORY OF THE CREW OF THE FLYING FORTRESS
WHICH CRASHED ON THE ARENIG 4th AUGUST 1943.
1st Lt JAMES N. PRATT, BOISE, IDAHO.
2nd Lt ALLAN M. BONER, TINLEY PARK, ILLINOIS.
2nd Lt WILLIAM A. BOWLING, COVINGTON, KENTUCKY.
T/Sgt FREDERIC J. ROYAR, QUEENS VILLAGE, NEW YORK.
S/Sgt WALTER J. JOHNSTON, FAYETTE, OHIO.
Sgt WALTER B. ROBINSON, SACRAMENTO, CALIFORNIA.
Sgt PHILLIP SIMONTE, HIGHLAND PARK, MICHIGAN.
Pfc ALFRED B. VAN DYKE, BROOKVILLE, PENNSYLVANIA.

TO THE CITIZENS OF PENLLYN, WALES, ON THE 50TH ANNIVERSARY OF THE ENDING
OF THE WAR, WE EXTEND OUR DEEPEST APPRECIATION FOR YOUR CONTINUED
REMEMBRANCE OF LT. ALLAN BONER, OF TINLEY PARK, AND THE AMERICAN CREW OF
HIS B17 THAT PERISHED ON ARENIG FAWR NEAR THE TOWN OF BALA ON AUGUST 4, 1943

WITH SINCERE BEST WISHES FROM THE VILLAGE GOVERNMENT
AND CITIZENS OF TINLEY PARK, ILLINOIS USA.

I DRIGOLION PENLLYN, CYMRU, TRA'N COFIO 50 MLYNEDD ER DIWEDD Y RHYFEL
ESTYNWN EIN GWERTHFAWROGIAD AM EICH COFFADWRIAETH PARHAOL I
LT. ALLAN BONER O PARC TINLEY, A'R CRIW AMERICANAIDD A FU FARW MEWN
AWYREN B17 AR FYNYDD YR ARENIG FAWR GER Y BALA, AWST 4YDD, 1943
GYDA DYMUNIADAU GORAU ODDIWRTH SENEDD A THRIGOLION PARC TINLEY, ILLINOIS USA.

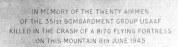

IN MEMORY OF THE TWENTY AIRMEN
OF THE 35st BOMBARDMENT GROUP USAAF
KILLED IN THE CRASH OF A B17G FLYING FORTRESS
ON THIS MOUNTAIN 8th JUNE 1945

CAPT. JOSEPH C. ROBINSON	S/SGT. SANTO A. CARUSO	SGT. JOHN D. LEASURE
CAPT. JOSEPH A. GLOVER	S/SGT. ROBERT E. SMITH	T/SGT. PAUL LUCYK
1st LT. HOWARD R. HIBBARD	M/SGT. JOHN Q. MONTGOMERY	T/SGT. MORRIS LEMEWSKI
T/SGT. KENNETH W. CRAUMER	1st LT. RICHARD E. HIGLEY	SGT. EDWIN R. BIRTWELL
T/SGT. LESTER A.F. RHEIN	S/SGT. TEED O. SMITH	SGT. SHELDON R. COONS
SGT. DAVID I. RAPOPORT	SGT. CAMILLE F. DEVANEY	SGT. BOYD P. DOBBS
T/SGT. MAX MARKSHEID	CPL. CALVERT G. POOL	

IN MEMORY
OF
THE US AIRFORCE CREW
KILLED ON THE GARN
FEBRUARY 1, 1945
CREW
N.B. SOWELL TEXAS
K.W. CARTY CALIFORNIA
W.H. CARDWELL UTAH
J.D. ARNOLD NORTH DAKOTA
R.M. AGUIRRE TEXAS

4th August 1943

'To the crew of the Flying Fortress.
that crashed on the summit
of Arenig Fawr'

War brought them – mist caught them.
Capsuled within foggy panes, we see them
hunched over dials and wavering needles
tapping the treacherous glass, gloved fingers
rapping the altimeter, sensing the danger.
Shock splinters their fear – a burst
of rock where no rock should have been
fisting its way through glass, flesh, metal.

And now the same mist shrouds them, a mesh
of droplets, beading pale foreheads, hands
grass and hard Welsh slate, clammy on leather
cold on the creaking fuselage; a grey wind
lifting torn shreds of aluminium, shards
scattered among the ancient mountain crags.

Eight crewmen, lost to Illinois, Kentucky
Ohio, California, New York, Michigan, Idaho
and Pennsylvania. We read their names, carved
on this slate and wonder who they were, or who
they might have been, had not their Fortress
fallen from that grim August sky – how far
they might have gone, how high have flown.

Derek J Thorp

**Memorial to B-17 crew on the summit of
Arenig Fawr.** *Ron Waldron*

**Plaque for the Arenig Fawr B-17 crew on
Old Town Hall, Bala.** *Don Konley*

**Memorial to the airmen on board the B-17
Fortress which crashed on Craig Cwm
Llwyd.** *David J Smith*

**Memorial to the crew of B-26 Marauder
44-68072, killed when their aircraft struck
the summit of Y Garn on 1st February 1945.**

Photographs on the opposite page:

**Recovery teams, including 34 MU, strain to
bring down wreckage from the Arenig B-17.**
Dick Morris

**Craig Cwm Llwyd, the last resting place of
B-17 Fortress 44-8639, just below the cliffs,
near centre of the photograph.** *Brian Jones*

Consolidated B-24J Liberator 42-99991, unassigned, on 7th January 1944

(see Chapter 1, page 9 onwards)

Boeing B-17G Fortress 42-31321. 'CC-M' of 390th BG 569th BS, on 8th July 1944

This aircraft was flying from North Africa to the UK when the crew became lost. Running short of fuel they spotted the small grass airfield at RAF Towyn, only used for such types as Lysanders and Henleys. On landing the Fortress soon ran out of runway and ran across a railway line where it collided with an air raid shelter. Here it caught fire, which was extinguished by the station fire party and the local NFS. The fifteen aircrew an board all survived.

Martin B-26G Marauder 44-68072, unassigned, 1st February 1945

This medium bomber left Florida towards the end of January 1945 with a crew of five. It flew across the Atlantic on the Southern Overseas Route via Natal in Brazil and Dakar in West Africa to Marrakesh and then to RAF St Mawgan in Cornwall.

At 1238 hours on 1st February the Marauder took off to fly to Burtonwood, the large USAAF base in Lancashire. It never arrived. In the afternoon, while driving at the bottom of the Llanberis Pass a Crosville bus driver heard an aircraft flying low in cloud, followed by an explosion. Explosions in a quarrying area due to blasting were common, and he did not report it until next day. The RAF Mountain Rescue Team were called out to an overdue aircraft report, and found that the Marauder had struck the very summit of 3,104 feet Y Garn which stands between the Nant Ffrancon and Llanberis Passes, with the loss of all the crew. Apparently, strong winds had affected the aircraft's track putting it into a collision course with Snowdonia.

A memorial plaque to the crew has now been placed in the wall of a layby in the Llanberis Pass.

Boeing B-17G Fortress 44-8639, of 511 Bomb Squadron, 351st Bomb Group, 8th June 1945

In June 1994, Mrs Muriel Andrew, of Cambridge, was on the last night of her holiday in Barmouth and set out for her usual after dinner walk down to the harbour with her son. 'Again we walked along the promontory of what I call the sea defence steps at the start of the estuary. On turning to look up the estuary to enjoy the wonderful view we saw a

Major G Wright Jnr, pilot of C-47 Skytrain (Dakota) 43-15105, examines the tailwheel of his aircraft abandoned near Conway on 29th March 1944. *USAF via David Roberts*

David Roberts with his haul of parts from the Dakota at Tremorfa Farm. *Glyn Davies*

Opposite: **Wreckage and one undercarriage assembly of the C-47 Skytrain hangs precariously above Llyn Dulyn.** *Walter W Harris*

strange 'something' descending from the sky until it was a little above house height, going across the river and disappearing behind some trees on the south side. This was approximately 9 pm. and we watched 'it' for about a minute. This 'something' appeared to be large, grey, silent, and very very eerie to watch. It reminded me of an old grey bomber coming in to land as it disappeared as silently and suddenly as it had appeared. It was a very thundery evening with an electric feel to the atmosphere with a high cloud cover *but this was definitely not a cloud.*'

Mrs Andrew sent this observation to the writer asking if I knew of any aircraft crash in the locality. She also sent a map showing the route taken by the apparition. It was flying directly towards Craig Cwm Llwyd.

Following the end of the war in Europe, hundreds of USAAF aircraft could be seen making their way to RAF Valley in Anglesey to refuel and leave Britain in stages for home. On the morning of 8th June 1945 B-17G Fortress 44-8639 took off from Polebrook in Northamptonshire. The pilot was 26 year old 1st Lieutenant Howard R Hibbard, with his crew and ten passengers on board, a total of 20 airmen. On reaching the North Wales coast near Barmouth just beneath a blanket of cloud at 900 feet, the pilot requested a QDM, or course to steer from RAF Valley at 0817 hours. This was given, but the pilot

P-47 41-6237 after a forced landing near Atcham. *David J Smith*

turned on a reciprocal heading and flew straight into the side of Craig Cwm Llwyd hidden in cloud. All twenty airmen were killed outright. Investigators concluded that the pilot came upon the inlet at Barmouth, and when inside realised his position and attempted a right turn to clear high ground. On a heading of 230 degrees the aircraft struck the mountain at 1100 feet, careered another 300 feet to where it burst into flames and exploded.

One researcher, Roy Handiforth, has ventured the theory that magnetic ores in the mountain affected the aircraft compass. A young local man, Matthew Rimmer, has spent a great deal of time researching this accident and has clarified some confusion in the B-17 serial, thought for years to be 44-6005, and in the number of airmen on board, which was, as the RAF Mountain Rescue Team from Llandwrog found, an unfortunate 20. Matthew has since erected a fine memorial plaque at the site.

THE TRANSPORTS

Douglas C-47A Skytrain 43-15105, unassigned, 29th March 1944

This aircraft had crossed the Atlantic on the Southern Overseas Route and on the early morning of 29th March 1944 took off from Marrakesh in Morocco and set course for RAF Valley, the western air terminal of the SOR. At 1129 hours the radio operator of the

C-47 contacted Valley and requested approach procedures. Nothing further was heard until 1220 hours when the C-47 crew advised that an error had been made. They had by-passed Valley and asked for a course to steer. This was given and the pilot advised to stay at 8,000 feet. At 1405 hours the RAF Mountain Rescue Team at RAF Llandwrog were notified that No.9 Group, which monitored aircraft movements in the region, had reported a faded plot in the Conway area. On reaching Conway Police Station the team was directed to a house two miles south overlooking the river, and from where the wrecked 'plane could be seen on the floodplain below Tremorfa Farm.

Here they found the pilot, Major G Wright Jnr, and his co-pilot. They advised the team that the three other crew members had baled out three minutes before at 9,000 feet, after the aircraft had started running out of fuel. The ROC Post at Tyn-y-Goes had plotted the C-47's course. It was ascertained that the others had landed safely near Caerhun and were taken to Conway Police Station.

In 1985 researcher David Roberts, with the aid of a mechanical digger, managed to recover many parts including an engine from the wet clay. He was able then to establish the serial number of the C-47 which had, up till then, eluded local researchers.

Above: **Wreckage of the P-47 Thunderbolt from Atcham which crashed on Mynydd Copog.** *David Roberts*

Below: **The engine of the P-47 from Atcham which crashed on Aran Fawddwy, now at foot of cliffs.** *Steve Roberts*

Douglas C-47B Skytrain 43-48473, of 27 Air Transport Group, 12th November 1944

On the morning of 12th November 1944, this aircraft took off from Le Bourget airport, Paris, which was by then back in Allied hands. It was carrying a cargo of mail and freight for the American base at Burtonwood, near Warrington. As the aircraft neared its destination a message was received that the airfield was fogbound, and intructions were given to divert to RAF Valley. The pilot, 2nd Lt W G Gough, acknowledged the message, but the aircraft never arrived. That afternoon, at 1500 hours an air reconnaissance of the Carneddau range was made by Flight Lieutenant T O Scudamore from RAF Llandwrog. As Mountain Rescue Team leader and medical officer he had been advised of a missing aircraft. There was no sign of the C-47.

Ten days later it was found by a Mountain Rescue party en route to the summit of Foel Grach with replacement batteries for the radio warning beacon at the summit. The Dakota had flown into the top of the cliffs above Llyn Dulyn with the loss of the crew of four, its tail overhanging the lake like a giant bird. Mail and personal effects was strewn everywhere.

Many years later the writer stood at the lakeside with only Peggy, a long-haired terrier, for company. The high black cliffs held a fairly large piece of the aircraft, as if teasing me to chance the climb. I was not tempted. It was a hostile place, and I was glad to escape. Later I would learn of several legends associated with the lake where, it is said, evil spirits preside on certain nights of the year.

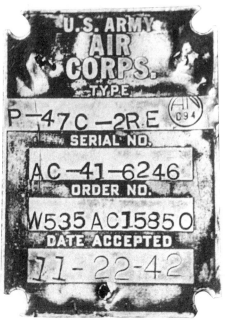

Captain Richard L Tannehill, who lost his life while flying a P-51 Mustang over Wales in 1945. *Charles E Konsler.*

Works plate of P-47 Thunderbolt on Aran Fawddwy. *David Roberts*

P-51 Mustang WD-C of 335th Fighter Squadron. Chuck Konsler on right with Mae-West on. *Charles E Konsler*

THE FIGHTERS

Republic P-47D Thunderbolt 42-75101, of 495th FTG, 4th May 1944

1st Lieutenant John W Beauchamp took off from USAAF Station 342 at Atcham, Shropshire in the early evening to fly a practice instrument and acrobatic mission over Wales. By 1930 hours the pilot had changed to the acrobatic phase with visibility at 2 miles, and cloud ceiling at 3,000 feet. As he flew down a valley, the pilot pulled the Thunderbolt up into a steep climb and rolled. During the second roll it went into a spin, which was recovered from, but at too low a height for the local terrain. The aircraft struck Mynydd Copog, near Mallwyd and Lt Beauchamp lost his life.

Republic P-47C Thunderbolt 41-6246, of 495th FTG, 16th September 1944

On this day Flight Officer Peter Quinci took off from Atcham for an interception and attack practice flight over Wales, and then vanished. Five days later, a shepherd advised RAF Llanbedr that he had found a recently crashed aircraft on Aran Fawddwy along with human remains. As the reported position was a rock face, the MR Team at RAF Llandwrog was asked to deal and were quickly on their way, picking up a police constable as guide at Dinas Mawddwy. On the mountain, the policeman confessed that he did not know exactly where the crash site was. The team then searched the rock face in a steady downpour and visibility of 10 to 50 yards, in vain. Darkness then intervened, so the Medical Officer called a halt to the search and a soaked team returned to base.

Next day they were able to find the shepherd who had discovered the crash. He led the team directly to the wreckage 100 feet below the summit of 2,970 feet Aran Fawddwy, again in adverse weather. Much of the aircraft was scattered down gullies on the east face. A take-off check list for a P-47C was found, confirming this as the missing Atcham aircraft. The pilot's remains were taken back to RAF Llanbedr and the team returned to Llandwrog after a very difficult operation in appalling weather.

North American P-51D Mustang 44-72340, of 335th Fighter Squadron, 4th Fighter Group, 17th May 1945

Captain Richard L Tannehill was flying over Wales in a formation of P-51s of the 335th Fighter squadron coded WD. Suddenly his Mustang dived out of formation and went into a steep spin, most likely caused by the pilot suffering oxygen starvation. The aircraft crashed on the lower slopes of Aran Fawddwy with no chance of survival. He was the last 335th pilot of the war to be killed.

Chapter Three

Luftwaffe Losses

Only three German aircraft came down within the boundaries of the Snowdonia National Park, the area of the first book. For the sake of completeness all those which came down on land in north-west Wales are now included, plus basic details of an air battle in October 1940.

Junkers Ju 88: 4U+BL, WNr not known, 3/Aufklarungsgruppe 123.

In the early morning of 7th September 1940 a Junkers Ju 88 took off from Paris-Buc airfield on a reconnaissance flight to north west England. In command was Oberleutnant Hans Kauter, acting as observer, while Leutnant Erich Bohle was the pilot. He was only called for duty when the usual pilot could not start the engines of the Junkers. Perhaps the usual pilot had the benefit of foresight.

They were spotted at 20,000 feet over Hoylake by an alert ROC observer. On hearing this report on his W/T in a Spitfire of No.7 OTU from Hawarden, Sergeant L S Pilkington made for the reported position. This veteran pilot of 73 Squadron attacked the Junkers with cannon fire.

Bohle recalls 'I heard a cry on the intercom "Spitfire! Spitfire!", and turned the Junkers to escape into the clouds. In this moment we got a heavy blow and the port motor was shot out of action by the cannonfire of the Spitfire. I was busy to get the Junkers in a horizontal flight position. It was very difficult to hold the aircraft with only the force of one engine. Expecting soon a landing I ordered to let out all the fuel. Sergeant Kobold (engineer) asked me if he should put out the machine gun too with which he had fired back at the Spitfire.' During this time Pilkington was chasing the enemy aircraft towards mid-Wales, firing at this elusive target at first from 400-450 yards, then later when it was down to 5,000 feet managed a burst at close range 50-100 yards, when the main damage was done. He last saw the Junkers diving into thick cloud at 4,000 feet.

Bohle – 'All then happened in seconds. As we lost heavily the altitude I asked Kobold to come up and he climbed immediately and stood behind the observer place. We were still in clouds without visibility. Seconds later I saw a little bit of ground, clouds all round, no space for landing. Only God could help us. It happened that the right wing of the aircraft touched the hill (Drum Ddu) and we crashed in the form of a pancake landing. With the crash I lost consciousness'.

All the crew were badly injured, but Kauter managed to inflate the life raft and help the three airmen into it. They had crashed in a most inhospitable place with no sign of habitation, so Kauter made his way slowly and painfully down the mountain until he came to a stream which he then followed. Four hours after the crash he staggered to the door of Gelli Ddolen farm, a few miles west of Mallwyd and raised the alarm to Idwal and Jane Jones. Many hours later the four airmen were being treated in Machynllech Hospital, the three at the crash site having been carried down on makeshift stretchers. All survived and were later transported to prisoner of war camps in Canada.

Junkers Ju88 on Drum Ddu, 7th September 1940. *S Burns*

An engine from the Junkers at Gelli Donen Farm. *S Burns*

Erich Bohle eventually settled in Venezuela. Hans Kauter came back to Wales in 1985 to thank those who helped him and his crew all those years before.

Later commissioned, Flight Lieutenant Leslie Pilkington DFM, of Hull, went missing when flying with 111 Squadron on 20th September 1942. His name is recorded on Panel 29 of the Runnymede Memorial.

Dornier 215 WNr 0023. VB+KK, 2/Aufklarungsgruppe 121

In October 1940, B Flight of 611 Squadron in their Spitfires were detached from Tern Hill to Ringway on a daily basis. Pilot Officer Dennis A Adams was one of these. At 1500 hours on the 21st the flight was scrambled to intercept an unidentified aircraft approaching Liverpool at 15,000 feet. Adams recalls 'My Flight Commander, Flight Lieutenant Stoddart reported B Flight airborne, at which time I was at 1,000 feet already and gave the old Merlin a bit more boost for good measure.

As I passed 15,000 feet I noticed flak bursting well above me. They were shooting at a Dornier 215 which was flying a line along the docks from Formby to Liverpool. At 28,000 feet the Do215 was about 2,000 feet below me so I made a quarter attack on the starboard side giving a two second burst from my guns. Oil and glycol poured from the starboard engine and the prop stopped. The oil covered my windscreen which I cleared by diving. The enemy aircraft was then above the Wirral and I tried to turn him to Hooton Park or Sealand by flying in front and waving and pointing. The pilot though kept on flying west and losing height until he made a forced landing in a small field. As it touched down it did a ground loop to starboard and then the port wing bashed into the west wall of the field.

I opened the hood and did a few slow circuits, and the pilot gave me some sort of salute, Nazi or otherwise I would not know.

Oberleutnant Hans Kauter, commander of Junkers Ju88 4U+BL. *Hugh Trivett*

A cheeky smile from Sergeant Leslie Pilkington, who downed the Junkers Ju88 4U+BL on Drum Ddu. *Russell Brown*

My last recollection is of the village Bobby in full uniform pedalling manfully up the rise to get to the wreck. I waggled my wings and set off back for Ringway'. The Dornier was on a reconnaissance flight to ascertain Luftwaffe damage on Liverpool in recent raids, and was piloted by Leutnant Rolf Book. It came down at Tyddyn Sais farm near Trawsfynydd. From the crew of four there was one fatality, Unteroffizier Gustav Pelzer, the engineer aged 26, who became the first enemy airman to be buried in north Wales, at Deiniol cemetery, Pwllheli. The other survivors were Feltwebeln Kurt Jensen and Hans Kuhl.

On an earlier excursion over Wales on 22nd July, Adams made a forced landing on the beach at Colwyn Bay in Spitfire N3062. The aircraft was pushed up the beach by the local populace to escape the incoming tide.

11th October 1940

On this evening, 'A' Flight Spitfires of 611 (West Lancashire) Squadron based at Ternhill, and 312 (Czech) Squadron Hurricanes from Speke were scrambled at 1715 hours to meet an incoming raid by Dornier 17s of Staffels 1, 2, & 3 from Kustenflieger Gruppe 606 coming in from the Irish Sea. The Spitfires gained height to 17,000 feet and gave battle giving the local populace in the area of Caernarfon Bay a much needed morale booster. Dornier 17Z 7T+EH (Werke Nr 2772) was shot up and ditched off Bardsey Island. While the commander, Leutnant zur See Jurgen von Krause, and two crew managed to climb into their dinghy, the harness of the pilot, Feldwebel Joseph Vetterl, caught in the aircraft and it took him down as it sank. The survivors were picked up by a Royal Navy trawler and taken to Holyhead. Pilot Officer J A Jaske's Hurricane was damaged in the engagement but he managed to return to base safely.

Dornier 17Z 7T+EK (Werke Nr 3475) was then promptly shot down into the sea off the

Leutnant Erich Bohle, pilot of Junkers Ju88 4U+BL. *Hugh Trivett*

Hans Kauter returns to Gelli Donen Farm in 1985 *Jan Heiland*

37

Lleyn peninsula by Sergeant K C Pattison, with the loss of all four crew. The body of Oberleutnant Fredrich Wilhelm Richter was later washed ashore and buried at Pwllheli. Sergeant Pattison was wounded during the engagement and disorientated. He crash-landed his Spitfire near Kidderminster and died of his wounds two days later.

The Spitfire pilots claimed another Dornier 17Z 7T+HH, which had been seen diving in flames near Capel Curig. An RAF team searching the area only found the cockpit canopy. The story of this aircraft was pieced together after the war, following a visit to Germany by journalist Ivor Wynne Jones. The wireless operator/gunner Feldwebel Hans Wilhelm Staas was giving a good account of himself when the Dornier was hit and the auxiliary 800 litre fuel tank caught fire. Oberleutnant zur See Heine, observer and commander gave orders to bale out. Staas got out with some difficulty due to the aircraft diving, but landed safely near Bethel. Unteroffizier Johannsen may have hit the tailplane and his parachute did not open. His body was found on the mountainside near Deiniolen, leaving an arms outstretched imprint seen for weeks afterwards. The Spitfire of Flying Officer T D Williams was damaged during the action, but he returned safely to base.

As the pilot, Leutnant der Reserve Kipmuller and the commander were preparing to abandon the Dornier, the fire suddenly blew out. The crew then made their way back to Brest on one engine and in freezing conditions without the canopy. Kipmuller survived the war but Heine, having had enough of aircraft transferred to U-Boats and lost his life in one off the coast of the USA.

Dornier Do 217 tail fin being guarded at Trawsfynnydd. *Mrs Menna W Haley*

Pilot Officer Dennis A Adams, of 611 Sqn, who shot down the Dornier Do 217 at Trawsfynnydd. *D A Adams*

Dornier Do 217 VB+KK at Trawsfynnydd. *Mrs Menna W Haley*

Pilot Officer Dennis A Adams (top left), with members of 611 Squadron. *D A Adams*

D.A.OXBY.   M.C.Shipard.

Pilot Officer Mervyn C Shipard and his observer Sergeant, later Pilot Officer, Douglas A Oxby, of 68 Sqn, who shot down Heinkel He111 F8+KR near Gwalchmai.
Merv Shipard

Dornier 17Z of Kustenflieger Gruppe 606.
H W Staas via Ifor Hughes

Heinkel He111H-5, WNr F4801, IT+EL. 3/KG28, 14th April 1941 on Llwydmor.
See Chapter 1

Heinkel He111H-6 WNr 0430, F8+KR. 7/KG40, 1st November 1941

Pilot Officer Mervyn C Shipard RAAF and Sergeant Douglas A Oxby were one of the crews of No 68 Squadron based at High Ercall, Shropshire, in 1941. During the period that No 456 Squadron at Valley were not operational while converting from Defiants to Beaufighters, High Ercall would send one Beaufighter each evening to Valley to cover the area. On the evening of 1st November, Shipard and Oxby were detailed for this task. On taking off from Valley at 2024 hours they patrolled the Bardsey Island area at 10,000 feet and were soon alerted to become stalkers, being taken over by Trewan Sands GCI radar at 2046. After several alterations of course, and once losing contact, Oxby picked up a return at maximum range. From there on he gave corrections to the pilot bringing them close to the quarry.

Shipard: 'On initial contact with the GCI station I was informed that the aircraft was classed as a Bogey, which meant that it would be up to me to identify it before taking any action. We spent about five minutes behind the aircraft, firstly from dead astern, then the starboard and port sides, but it was not until I got directly below that I recognised the elliptical cut outs at the wing roots

Merv C Shipard (right) and radio observer Doug Oxby with their Beaufighter 'Slippery Ship II' at Castel Benito airfield, Tripoli, in May 1943, an airfield visited in an Avro York by the writer on the way to do National Service in West Africa in 1947. *M C Shipard*

Wing Commander E C (Ted) Wolfe, and Pilot Officer A E Ashcroft with their Beaufighter X8251. *Mrs Judith Wolfe*

Photographs on the opposite page:

Wreckage of Heinkel He111 being inspected by Pilot Officer A E Ashcroft (left) on Pwllheli beach. *Mrs Judith Wolfe*

Wg Cdr E C Wolfe, P/O A E Ashcroft, and Heinkel pilot Stabsfw Dirk Hofkes. *Mrs Judith Wolfe*

Photographs on this page:

Aviation historian Bob Roberts with a propeller from the Heinkel on Pwllheli beach in 1995. *R E Roberts.*

Luftwaffe graves plot at Deiniol Cemetery, Pwllheli, since removed to Cannock Chase. L-R 1st row: Uffz G Pelzer 21.9.40; Uffz H Johannsen 7.10.40; Oblt F W Richter 7.10.40. 2nd row: Unknown buried 24.6.41; Fw W Franke 22.7.41; Fw H Vogt 30.7.42; Obgf H von Sheven 6.6.46; killed on a bicycle as a PoW. *John Wright*

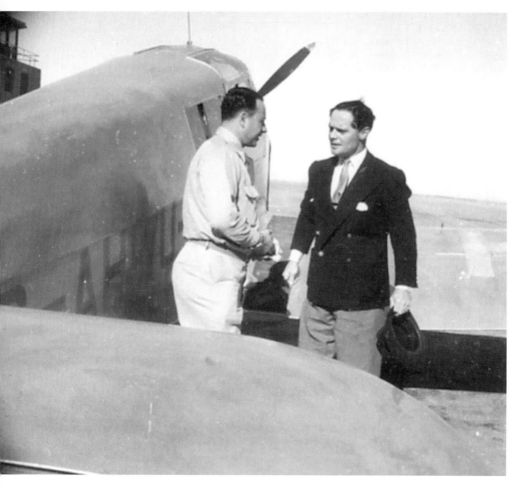

Old comrades reminisce; Ted Wolfe and Douglas Bader in 1948 alongside Percival Proctor G-AHWU. *Mrs Judith Wolfe*

(ie He111) which was good enough for me. At a height of 12,700 feet and from dead astern I opened fire at 300 feet range giving a two second burst. The starboard of the enemy aircraft immediately caught fire and then the whole of the interior seemed to catch fire. It fell steeply to port and spiralled down until it disappeared in cloud at 7,000 feet. Then the undersurface of our aircraft was lit by an explosion below the cloud and later we saw the enemy aircraft burning on the ground.'

In fact the Heinkel crashed at Bwlch-y-Fen, near Gwalchmai at 2305 hours with the loss of the entire crew, Leutnant G Leins, Unteroffizieren A Tepe, G Fischer and Gefreiter R Terstegen. The body of Leutnant Leins was never found. Shipard visited the crash site next morning and apologised to the occupants of a large house nearby for causing all the windows to be blown out. There was little left of the Heinkel. Bombs on board exploded on impact leaving a large crater and little else. On closer inspection, Pilot Officer Shipard was shown the tail wheel which had a Dunlop tyre, made in England.

Heinkel He111H-5, WNr 3962, F8+LW. 12/KG40, 30th July 1942

Wing Commander E (Ted) C Wolfe was a distant relative of General James Wolfe of Quebec fame, and a veteran of the Battle of Britain. On the night of 6/7th May 1941 he and his turret gunner, Sergeant A E Ashcroft, shot down a Junkers Ju88 of KG2/106 (M2+CK), while Wolfe was the CO of No 141 (Defiant) Squadron. The aircraft dived into the ground and exploded at Newlands, Stirlingshire. The German crew of four all baled out successfully. On visiting the site next day, Wolfe and Ashcroft were subjected to abuse from the farmer whose crop had been damaged, so made a hasty retreat.

The night of 29/30th July 1942 found Wolfe, now CO of No 456 (RAAF) Squadron at RAF Valley, along with Pilot Officer A E Ashcroft in Beaufighter RX-A (X6251) patrolling over Bardsey Island at 10,000 feet. At 0112 hours they were taken over by Trewan Sands GCI radar and given a course of 280 degrees to fly. At 0125 hours Ashcroft observed two blips on his radar screen and directed Wolfe towards them. As they neared the first aircraft Wolfe identified it as a Junkers Ju88, but they were spotted and the enemy turned out to be an extremely experienced pilot who could turn inside the Beaufighter and managed to escape. Later it would bomb gasworks in Birmingham. In the meantime Wolfe and Ashcroft latched on to the other blip.

This second blip turned out to be an Orleans based Heinkel He111 coded F8+LW of 12/KG40, with a load of high explosives and incendiaries loaded for an attack on Birmingham. Wolfe: 'I closed in on the enemy aircraft, which was jinking about making Rate 1, 50 degree turns. Closing in, I obtained a visual at 2,000 feet range, identifying machine as He111 from the engine exhausts, which were most apparent. With the enemy aircraft now descending slightly, I closed in at around 270-280 knots to 250 yards, gave slight port deflection and opened fire for two seconds. I closed in to 150 yards and fired again for one second. There was no return fire as the gunner had been killed by the first burst. As the He 111 skidded off to port and jettisoned its bomb load, I broke away to starboard and fired again for two seconds, then broke away violently to avoid a collision. This burst resulted in bright flashes from the fuselage with pieces falling off the enemy aircraft. A large dark object passed beneath my aircraft, slightly to port. This is now presumed to be the port engine as this has not been found in the wreckage.'

Owen Thomas had just beached his dinghy after fishing with another man off Pwllheli when the flaming Heinkel fell out of the sky onto the beach. Shortly afterwards they heard shouting from seawards 'Kamarad, Kamarad!'. The other man said to take no notice, it was a German, let him drown. However, to Owen Thomas it was still a human drowning out there and he launched the dinghy and they rowed out to the source of the cries. Here they found the wireless operator, Unteroffizier Johann Hesketh, with both legs broken. They hauled him aboard with great difficulty and rowed him to shore where he was handed over to the authorities to be taken to hospital under guard. The parachute of the observer, Feldwebel Horst Vogt, snagged the Heinkel's tail on baling out and he was carried down with the aircraft, along with the already dead gunner, Gefreiter Heinz Heferle. The pilot, Stabsfeldwebel Dirk Hofkes, managed to bale out successfully and was soon rounded up by the many military about, stirred up like a hornets nest by all the battle noise from the heavens. Next day Wing Commander Wolfe and his observer visited the vanquished survivors in hospital.

Ted Wolfe was awarded the DFC in 1942 by King George VI, and later the Norwegian Cross by King Haakon. The latter was in recognition of Wolfe's work at Oslo airport to reactivate the Norwegian Air Force following the German capitulation.

He survived the war but died in 1994 from the unfortunate results of a stroke. He was a warm and friendly person with a keen sense of humour, a joy for a researcher to talk to. It was a privilege to have known him. Sadly, his observer, Pilot Officer Ashcroft, was killed a few weeks before war ended in a Mosquito over Germany.

At the time of writing, the recovered Heinkel engine is in Caernarfon Air Museum.

Chapter Four

The Whirlybirds, Cessna and a Microlight

Hughes 269C G-CHIC, 12th November 1979
This helicopter was on hire to MANWEB for the purpose of checking high voltage electricity lines in North Wales. The pilot was Captain D McGillivray, with MANWEB engineer David Booth on board to carry out observation on the lines. On arrival near Betws-y-Coed the pilot elected to land on a rocky outcrop, a clearing in an extensively wooded area, for a short break. When it was time to take off again the engine took several attempts to start. On moving off after hovering, the pilot shouted 'there's something wrong with the controls'. They drifted down into the trees and crashed. David Booth was not badly injured, and a party of Royal Artillery junior soldiers on exercise were swiftly on the scene to extricate and carry the pilot to a waiting ambulance. Unfortunately Captain McGillivray had sustained a fractured skull and died on arrival at hospital. He was not wearing a protective helmet.

Air Accidents Investigation Branch of the DoT found that the engine of the helicopter was only producing 72% power, and was the primary cause of the accident.

Gazelle HT3 XX374, 2FTS, 20th April 1983
This RAF helicopter was being flown on an authorised flight in the mountains of Snowdonia. The pilot was a helicopter instructor with a commonwealth student pilot on board. The aircraft was observed to fly very low near a Snowdon Mountain Railway train. Later it came over the summit and down the eastern side of Snowdon following the Miners Track, where it flew over a school party, again at an extremely low level, after which it collided with the mountain. The two pilots were thrown out and had almost immediate attention from adults in the party, but to no avail. Both pilots lost their lives.

Enstrom F-28C G-BGSN, 12th June 1991
The lake of Marchllyn Mawr on Elidir Fawr was deepened in the 70's as the upper part of the massive pumped-storage power station within the mountain near Llanberis. An Enstom helicopter was flown to the lake by pilot Bob Blackwell to make a recruiting video for the construction industry. Cameraman Chris Hall climbed aboard below the dam and they flew to hover at 60 feet above the western corner of the dam. They then set off eastwards across the lake. Suddenly a violent downdraught swept down from the peaks and, like a giant hand, seized the helicopter and pushed it down to the waters below, although the pilot increased the engine rpm to maximum.

The pilot however kept his cool and settled it squarely onto the surface in a downwind ditching, switching off the engine and master electrics switch on contact. As it sank he hauled himself and the cameraman out through the righthand door, and they swam to the shore. The 1,400 megawatt power station was shut down for a while as a precaution. Thankfully, the crew suffered no after effects.

The writer had traversed the drained lake bed in 1976 while involved with making a film for an Associate Section of PO Electrical Engineers competition. I recall someone saying 'We will only be able to make this journey in a submarine next year'. A helicopter was not envisaged.

Westland Wessex XR524, 22 Sqn C Flight, 12th August 1993. see Chapter 13

Hiller UH-12E4 Soloy
G-BTJE, 15th March 1995

This helicopter was contracted to the Snowdonia National Park Authority for three days in March 1995. Piloted by Peter Schofield, it was carrying materials with underslung loads for new footbridges being built close to Aber Falls. At 1100 hours it collided with 132,000 volt electricity cables and crashed in trees alongside the Afon Rhaeadr Fawr. The helicopter was badly broken up, but the pilot survived though severely injured. The trees may well have softened the fall.

The AAIB investigation found that witnesses had observed the pilot making a left turn towards the pick-up point when the helicopter's nose suddenly dropped so that the tail boom struck the power cables. The pilot recalled seeing three ducks flying towards the cables, but nothing else; indeed one mallard was found dead in the wreckage. It was considered that the sudden dip of the nose of the helicopter may well have been due to an avoiding manoeuvre, causing contact with the cables. The pilot had flown over 5,000 hours in helicopters.

G-CHIC Hughes 269C near Betws y Coed.
North Wales Weekly News

Gazelle HT3 XX374 on an open day at RAF Valley. *David Roberts*

47

Chaser S447 G-MVDO, 1st July 1995

Graham Garnham, the pilot of this microlight aircraft took off from Waverton near Chester at 0620 hours accompanied by a friend in another microlight. The intention was to fly along the coast at a height of 1,500 feet to Caernarfon, land and refuel before returning. Overcast skies started to break up at Conwy, though there was a south-east wind blowing off the mountains to his left. As he passed Penmaenmawr the pilot radioed to his friend, two miles behind, that the air was calmer ahead. When the second pilot reached Bangor, he attempted to call his colleague on the radio to no avail. He turned back towards Llanfairfechan. Just before the town he saw the other red microlight on Glan-y-mor Elias beach. It was soon determined that the pilot had been killed.

The AAIB investigation along with the manufacturer, found no fault with the aircraft structure, and that the engine was producing a high degree of power at impact. The pilot's helmet was found some distance from the wreckage. The RAF School of Aviation Medicine were asked to examine the helmet. They came to the conclusion that it came off on impact and rolled away. However it had been modified internally to hold the radio microphone and as such reduced the ability to protect the wearer in case of impact. While this may have been the cause of the pilot losing his life, the reason for the microlight descending was not determined. The second aircraft had flown the same route and had evidently coped with the turbulence encountered in the airflow from the mountains.

Robinson R22 Beta G-IFOX
3rd August 1997

This flight was to continue training in mountain flying techniques. The pilot approached the knife edge ridge between Crib Goch and Crib-y-Ddysgl at 3,200 feet and brought the helicopter to the hover with the right skid touching the slope. There it was held in a 10 knot cross wind for five seconds when a

Gazelle XX374 wreckage on Snowdon.
David Roberts

48

sudden strong gust of wind caught it and blew it over. The pilot and passenger, who had been wearing full seat belts, quickly vacated the helicopter without injury, and were helped by climbers and staff from the nearby Snowdon summit cafe. See back cover photo.

Low on Lift: Enstrom F-28C, which ditched in Marchlyn Mawr, was rebuilt and re-registered as G-OIGS. It awaits its whirly bits at Sywell. *W W (Bill) Taylor*

Aerospatiale AS355F1 G-WIRE
9th September 1997
This helicopter was being used for carrying materials over the high ground section of the 400,000 volt National Grid power lines in Snowdonia. At 4.20 pm a rotor blade hit and cut one of the lines during gusty conditions. The pilot managed to make a controlled landing with no injury close to the Roman Road from Roe Wen to Aber.

These operations in proximity to power lines were potentially hazardous. In May of the year a Bristow's helicopter dropped a load of scaffolding poles 600 feet into a field near Llanfairfechan during these activities. These accidents followed the crash of a helicopter which hit power lines near the Aber Falls in March 1995, listed earlier.

Cessna 152 G-BIIJ, 23rd May 1998
After obtaining a reasonable weather forecast for a flight from Leicester Airport to Blackpool, and with due authorisation, the pilot of this aircraft took off with one passenger at 0925 hours. Later on, Manchester Approach Control advised the pilot of deteri-

orating weather there and in the north-west generally, and advised diverting. At this time the Cessna was tracked as being 8 miles northwest of Shawbury. The pilot stated he was turning onto 270 degrees at 1029 hours to fly to the coast. With no further radio contact, the Cessna was tracked on radar with an increasingly concerned controller trying to establish the altitude of the aircraft flying towards the Welsh mountains, until 1115 hours when radar contact ceased.

At this time, climbers on 3,008 feet Tryfan heard an aircraft approaching in poor visibility, followed by the sound of a crash below them. A doctor in the party which found the wreckage pronounced the occupants dead at the scene at 2,540 feet on the east face of Tryfan. The subsequent investigation found that the pilot and passenger had ingested cannabis and amphetamines recently. The former may have affected the pilot's reasoning and decision making, and the latter could have made him overconfident. Also, when advised to divert, the pilot took this to mean divert round the weather rather than land at another airfield. He could have also returned to Leicester when the weather began to deteriorate, the usual course of action.

Hiller UH-12E4 Soloy, G-BTJE near Aber Falls. *Gerallt Jones*

Chaser S447, G-MVDO being given a preflight check by its owner. *John Huxley via John C S Jones*

Aerospatiale AS355F1, G-WIRE, by the Roman Road above Llanfairfechan. *Author*

Cessna 152, G-BIIJ, near the summit of Tryfan. *Ogwen Valley Mountain Rescue Team*

Part II

THE
SURVIVORS

**The pilot and observer walked away from
Fairey Firefly WJ153 when it crashed during a
forced landing (Chapter 10).** *Alan Hawkins*

Chapter Five

The Bells of Aberdovey
(Wellington X9666)

One of the many legends of Wales tells of the rich land of Gwaelod to the west of Aberdovey. It was below sea level, so was protected by stout sea-walls, the maintenance of which was the responsibility of two brothers. Prince Teithrin watched over the north wall, and lazy Prince Seithenin the south. One night a terrible storm arose. The well maintained north wall held, but the sea started to breach the south wall while Prince Seithenin, and his men, caroused in his castle. His brother was unable to motivate him and the sea rushed in and drowned the land. Prince Teithrin rescued Seithenin's daughter, the fair Rhonwen, just in the nick of time.

It is said that the bells of a drowned church can sometimes be heard swinging with the incoming tide. Perhaps they now also toll for airmen who lost their lives on a nearby mountain.

Sergeant Peter North had completed training as an air bomber in Canada and, on returning to Britain, attended an advanced flying course at RAF Penrhos with night flying from Llandwrog. In November 1943 he was posted to No 21 OTU at RAF Moreton in Marsh in Gloucestershire. Here everyone was crewing up with other airmen who would serve together in operational squadrons. Peter North reflected that what you were really doing was choosing the people you were likely to die with, given the losses on bomber squadrons. He teamed up with Warrant Officer Goronwy Roberts, affectionately known as Robbie – a good and cautious pilot, Sergeant Trevor Freeman, navigator, Sergeant Tom Briggs, wireless operator/air gunner, and Sergeant Arthur Mundell, rear gunner. They made several cross-country flights together sounding out each other's skills in the process.

The First Crash

On 18th December the crew took off in Wellington DV808 for a long cross-country flight. Straight away they were into low cloud and the wireless operator was kept busy requesting QDMs for position. It was at this time they must have missed a recall signal because thicker cloud was moving in. However, near York, the aircraft emerged from the mat of cloud. North asked the skipper for permission to go into the front turret, and proceeded to go through first the canvas, then the turret doors. He informed the pilot that he was rotating the turret, as this would alter the airflow, and checked it out. On completion he reversed the entry sequence and stepped back into the fuselage, though his feet found just empty space. The entrance hatch had opened while he was in the turret, and now he hung half-in and half-out of the aircraft at 12,000 feet. It was freezing cold. Eventually he managed to pull himself up and close the hatch. The pilot was livid, not having any communication for several minutes and wondering what North was playing at. That was the first incident: there were more to come.

They then turned for Flamborough Head, where commenced a 20 mile wide channel out over the North Sea and then south to the Wash, reserved for training flights. North had a fine pinpoint for the Head, and he then sighted a convoy. A few moments later flashes came up at them – they were being fired at! The pilot shouted 'Fire the colours of the day'. This was promptly done with a Verey pistol, but it made no difference, they were the centre of unwelcome attention. The pilot called on the intercom 'I'm going down – strap in', and proceeded to dive down until they were at 5,000 feet and away from the convoy. The wireless operator reported their position to base, standard procedure, but received no reply. Nothing could be found wrong with the radio, so it was assumed that the trailing aerial has been lost in the dive. The aircraft was now in cloud again, but they saw the Norfolk coast fleetingly on descending further, though were not able to identify any landmark. Robbie then announced 'I've just picked up a homing signal' on their instrument landing system radio. When they were well down the cone for landing, the signals suddenly cut off, presumably the originating airfield believing an enemy intruder was using it. At this moment Briggs informed the pilot that he had picked up the tail-end of a message with their callsign diverting them to High Ercall in Shropshire. The crew set the new course and thundered through the murk, climbing to 5,000 feet to be safe for any intrusion into Wales.

Next the IFF set (Identification Friend or Foe) started squeaking into the intercom for all to hear, indicating they were approaching barrage balloons. The pilot turned the Wellington through 180 degrees, but the warning signals did not go away. The crew seemed to be in a box from which they could not escape. After wriggling this way and that they finally succeeded, only to find they were quite lost. Everyone was anxiously scanning the cloud for a break. Roberts asked North to request help on the 'Darky' set, from any ROC post in the area, but this brought no result. Suddenly the pilot called that he could see a gap in the cloud and shot down through it only to find they were surrounded by mountains. They flew up a valley at low level and found the far end closed. Roberts managed to turn around and then noticed the fuel state was low, with only the nacelle tanks supply left. On finding a green patch he decided to put the aircraft down and ordered the crew to crash positions. Peter North had his fingers on the fire-extinguisher buttons. They made a wheels-down landing at 1550 hours, but ploughed through a stout hedge and the landing gear collapsed. Then the

starboard wing was torn off, and then stillness. North hit the buttons and the engines were immediately covered in foam. The crew were uninjured and evacuated the aircraft quickly.

No-one could find a cigarette to steady their nerves, which is just as well with petrol and oil about.

Sergeant Peter North returns to Wales at the presentation of Scouts Bronze Medal to David Hughes. Mr North senior far left.
Ray & Mrs C M Webb

When local people arrived they found that they were on a golf course five miles from Huddersfield. The practise bombs were still on board and North had to crawl under the Wellington where the bomb-bay doors had been ripped off and slowly secure the bomb safety pins, which was hair-raising, but managed all but one. An Army contingent arrived to guard the aircraft and transport them to their barracks in an old mill. While they were eating dinner, black pieces were noticed in the mashed potato. Scuffling noises on the rafters were identified as rats running about, so their appetites evaporated!

On going out for a drink, the first pub they came to was called, astonishingly, 'The Wellington', where they were not allowed to buy any drinks, but were plied with them by the locals until recollections fade. After the return to base a Court of Inquiry blamed Warrant Officer Roberts for the forced landing, clearly the scapegoat, for without radio contact they did not know the wind had shifted from north to south and put them 120 miles off track. Roberts was posted away to become a staff pilot, and later commissioned to Pilot Officer.

The Second Crash

The new pilot assigned to the crew was Flying Officer C R Amos, from Argentina, who had already completed a tour on operations. They made several local flights to integrate the new crew member into the team, mainly circuits and bumps. This was not quite so chummy an arrangement with them since the rest were all Sergeants and, in any case, the crew were still put out at losing a pilot with whom they had worked so well. Their old skipper always had a little get together in a village pub once a week as a sort of thank you for getting through it. A room was booked on 31st December for a last gathering with Robbie and for a group photograph. But first they had another cross-country flight to make.

Warrant Officer (Sergeant at the time) Arthur Mundell. *A Mundell*

Sergeant Tom Briggs. *Mrs Holloway (sister)*

At 1005 hours on the 31st they took off in Wellington X9666 and headed for a bombing range where a clover leaf pattern was flown for the release of practise bombs. They then flew west on a typically December day with the ground all the same colour, a sort of greyish-green. The clouds were 10/10ths stratocumulus with an 8,000 feet base, now lowering. The pilot said he was going to try to get above them. The engines were not up to much, not having had a major overhaul since the aircraft had come off operations in 1941. They seemed to growl in protest as altitude was increased, and at 10,000 feet the port engine started to ice up. They dropped down below the cloud for an hour. Then they ran into cloud again which followed them as altitude was lost to 5,000 feet. They could not climb above it because of the faulty engine, and could not descend further for they were over the Welsh mountains with a safety height of 4,000 feet. At this time Briggs obtained radio bearings and Freeman made a small alteration to their course to a turning point at Towyn from this. After a while the pilot asked for an ETA (Estimated Time of Arrival) for the coast. The navigator made a quick calculation from his running plot and said 'one minute from now skipper'.

'I've just seen the sea' announced the pilot, 'I'm going down'. North had been clambering about the aircraft including the bomb aimer's position trying to see if he could pick up any sign of the ground through the cloud. Following the pilot's call he climbed up into the co-pilot's seat and leaned over to see out of the port side. In the Wellington the pilot was perched high up and had a better view forward than anyone else. Amos put the nose down and they picked up speed. None of the crew were strapped in, being unnecessary for straight and level flight. Peter North takes up the story 'I was still in the co-pilot's seat as we rushed downwards though the cloud, tilted at quite a sharp angle. I couldn't

Sergeant Trevor Freeman. *Peter North*

Rescuer King's Scout David Owain Hughes of the 1st Dovey Group. *The Scout Association*

see the sea, and everything was floating about me, including my maps which I grabbed at. I looked at the instrument panel and saw the airspeed indicator showing 242 knots (280 mph), and began to feel a bit worried. The skipper was an experienced pilot with many flying hours and a tour behind him, and I was only a sprog Sergeant. But I was uneasy, and felt I ought to say something about him slowing down a bit. I hesitated, you don't query a skipper's decision, after all it isn't a committee actually flying the aircraft. I turned to look at him and made motions with my hands as I did so – UP – UP – UP, but did not have time to say anything. As I turned my head to the left to speak to him something flickered in the corner of my eye. I turned my head towards it as the clouds drew apart. Directly in front of us was the biggest hill I have ever seen in my life, all grey-green, with tattered shreds of cloud just clearing from it. We had broken through the cloud base. I knew it was too late to do anything, I just shouted to the skipper 'UP – UP, the hill man – the hill, LOOK – OUT!'

What the pilot had seen though a hole in the clouds was the Dovey estuary, to the north-west, at full tide but not the mist shrouded hills beyond. I whipped my feet upon to the instrument panel and braced myself. With my left hand I jerked down the escape hatch release over my head and put both arms in front of my head to protect it. This was all standard training stuff instilled in us that we had done on the ground. There was a terrific crash. My legs were jarred off the instrument panel and I was fighting like mad to get them back as we shot about 600 yards further, through hedges of rammed earth, before we hit another hill. My whole body went forward, my eyes were open and I saw the bombsight come flying through the

air right across my leg. The starboard wing hit and, as we slewed round in a ground loop, I was shot like a bullet from a gun into the space where the escape hatch had been. Unfortunately, I didn't go right through but jammed mid-thigh. The rest of my body went on and downwards, leaving my legs inside the aircraft.

It was a tremendous shock. I don't remember anything else until I awoke to the smell of burning. The aircraft was stationary and upright and I was hanging head downwards on the pilot's side. I could hear the flames and smell the putrid smoke. I thought I must get out of this, I must get down. By forcing the palms of my hands against the side of the aircraft and pushing myself back I got them on the edge of the escape hatch, which was incredibly painful. I don't think I screamed, but I lifted myself up with my arms so that my legs were free from the inferno inside. This was pure fear, I had no wish to be toasted alive. Later, I woke up to find I was lying facing the rear of the Wellington. I turned my head as far as I could and I saw my feet. I'd lost my boots somehow and could see my heels. Only a contortionist could do it in that position.

I lifted up my head and looked around, though I had only half an eye to see with. My right eye was completely shut, and my left had a huge flap of skin hanging over it. Wherever I turned my head all I could see were flames, great big orange-salmon covered things. I thought if I stay here I'm done for. Here I was lying in front of the port wing, and the fuel tanks were close by in the wing, so if I was going to get away it had to be now. I put my head down, dug my elbows into the ground and hitched myself forward, hitch after hitch after hitch. I crawled right through

the flames. When I was right underneath the motor a great gout of flaming stuff dropped on me, petrol or oil – I don't know which. I just kept on going and somehow got out at the trailing edge of the wing. About then Arthur Mundell came rushing up and asked 'Pete can you walk?'

I was really upset by this question. I swore very hard and told him if I could walk I would have been instead of crawling. I don't remember much after that'.

Ensconced in the rear turret, Sergeant Arthur Mundell was viewing the world they had flown over, which was very little since they were mostly in cloud. The pilot announced he was going down below cloud and over the sea to escape the icing conditions which prevailed. Suddenly Mundell saw the ground hurtling by just beneath the aircraft but, as he made a grab for his oxygen mask to shout a warning, they hit. There was

Rescuers and survivors meet by the crash site of Wellington X9666 in September 1992. L-R Alun & Lewis Jones, Llew Hughes, Peter North, David Hughes, Arthur Mundell, and Emrys Jones (Mayor of Aberdovey). *Author*

Commonwealth War Graves Commission headstone of Sergeant Tom Briggs at Worcester. *Peter North*

a tremendous crash and prolonged buffeting. He managed to hit everything in the turret with his face including the gun sight. Then it stopped and he thought 'That wasn't too bad, but I'd best get out quick, it will burn'. He flipped the turret open but it was it was jammed fore and aft, and was confronted by a mass of twisted geodetic metal, leaving little space between. With his Irvin jacket, Mae West, and parachute harness it looked an impossibility to escape, but fear accelerated his progress and he shot through and out. He found that the tail section had broken off on impact. 'The scene which confronted me was akin to Dante's Inferno. The main fuselage was a veritable furnace, blazing from end to end. Ammunition was going off in all directions, joined by various pyrotechnic flares. The navigator and wireless operator were in the fuselage and must have been killed on impact.

I found Peter North outside the aircraft and pulled him away some distance to protect him from flying debris and ammunition. He said 'My legs are like chicken sticks'. I next found Flying Officer Amos some way ahead of the aircraft, having gone through the windscreen. I could only recognise him by the fact that he was the only one of us with a moustache. He was still alive, so I covered him with a parachute. The weather was foul, driving rain and a heavy mist. Then I saw a boy of about fourteen down the hill and stood up and waved to him. He rushed up, obviously pleased to see any survivors out of the inferno.

David Hughes, a King's Scout of the 1st Dovey Sea Scouts, was sitting on his bicycle on the road just east of the town when he heard an aircraft approaching from across the estuary. A Wellington bomber roared alarmingly low above him, heading for the range of hills which rose sharply behind Aberdovey. Knowing it must crash, he headed up a sparsely populated valley climbing onto the bare mountain, known locally as Ffrith Caenewydd, 700 feet above. Here he viewed the fiercely burning bomber, but was

heartened by the sight of two airmen, the one standing beckoning to him. On reaching Mundell he helped to drag North over an earth wall to give some protection from the ammunition, heat, and weather. He stayed at his post until help arrived. David's brother Llew, who was close behind stayed with the pilot. Two other brothers, Alun and Lewis Jones from a nearby farm, Esgair Gefeiliau, came on the scene, along with Emrys Jones who ran down the mountain to raise the alarm. When Dr Wright arrived he gave the pilot a morphine injection, and told Llew to see that no other medication was given on the scene. Next, Alun and Lewis Jones brought along a cart to wheel the survivors to the road. Soon they were on their way by ambulance to Towyn Cottage Hospital. On arrival Peter North sat bolt upright and announced 'I must have a piss, I must have a piss!' to the amusement of all the nurses waiting there.

The pilot, Flying Office Amos, did not survive. Peter North did, though badly injured and to this day he walks with the aid of a stick. Arthur Mundell who was 19 years old was back on duty three weeks later. He joined a crew captained by Flight Lieutenant Muggeridge and completed a tour of operations with Nos 70 and 37 squadrons. He stayed in the Royal Air Force for almost 37 years including during the Korean War.

David Hughes was awarded the Scouts Bronze Medal for his high standard of courage, endurance, and devotion to duty.

Their original pilot, now Pilot Officer Goronwy Roberts, was stationed at No.3(O) Advanced Flying Unit, Halfpenny Green (also known as Bobbington), on 30th May 1945, a few weeks after the war in Europe was over. He was given permission to land there in Anson DG799 at 1100 hours. However, on final approach his Anson was in collision with Oxford HM482. The two airmen in each aircraft lost their lives.

On 27th September 1992 the writer met the Wellington survivors and rescuers and we visited the spot where the Wellington burnt out. My high regard for those airmen has never wavered, the survivors, and those who did not. Like Prince Teithrin in legend, they are not forgotten.

A Wellington (L4253) crew parade before take-off. *Vickers*

Chapter Six

A Bridge Too Far

(Anson N4980)

Two new arrivals at RAF Penrhos in April 1942 were Sergeants Les Cooper and T J Crilly, who had just completed training as observers in Canada. At that time observers carried out the duties of navigating and bomb aiming, so some of the flights were over Hell's Mouth, aiming smoke bombs at targets in the bay. As night flying was carried out at RAF Llandwrog, they moved over there and prepared for a flight on 20th April in Anson N4980. The crew were to be pilot Sergeant C C Symonds, wireless operator Sergeant D J Stokes, and three observers on board to familiarise them with some of the beacons and other lights still to be found as navigational aids. However, one observer found the proximity of the comparative high-life of Caernarvon too much and vanished in that direction, leaving Cooper and Crilly as the passengers for the flight: the navigation was to be done by the pilot.

On take-off, Crilly sat by the pilot on the folding seat, and Cooper behind in the navigator's position. The pilot flew them as far as the sweep of Llandudno Bay, just made out in the near dark. On turning for base the two observers changed places and, peering into the night, later passed over a bridge standing out above water. 'Menai Bridge!' said the pilot over the intercom, making a small course correction. Some minutes later Cooper suddenly saw the vague shape of a mountain peak looming out of the darkness, and they struck, the Anson cartwheeling up the slope. Cooper's first thought was FIRE! and quickly vacated the wreckage, crawling on hands and knees. Stokes, the wireless operator, released the pilot, hanging upside down in his harness, and assisted him out. Crilly, a Scot, had been thrown against the

navigator's table and his chest crushed. He asked Stokes for his rosary from an inside pocket. Stokes found the beads and placed them in the observer's hands, and he died fingering the rosary.

Stokes was a tower of strength, releasing the dinghy and inflating it to make a shelter from the biting wind at this altitude – in excess of 2,500 feet. Not only that, he succeeded in finding a fuel tank tap and got a fire going with the petrol and pieces of aircraft. Symonds was heavily concussed and wandered around asking 'Where is the axe?'. He could not even recall having taken off. The three survivors were on the mountain with a blazing fire all night and no one saw them. During the night Cooper set off to walk down the hill. There were darker patches even in the black of night, and he thought they looked like sheer drops, so he turned back to the warmth and comfort of the fire. In fact they were on the slopes of Foel Fras and he had reached the edge of the 600 feet cliffs above Llyn Dulyn. Soon after dawn an aircraft flew over and the wireless operator asked if he should fire the Verey pistol. Cooper replied 'They will have seen us, but let it off anyway'. Later they learned that base had organised a square search from the air, and *had not* seen them before the flare was fired. After this another aircraft came over low and dropped a parcel on a home made parachute. However the parachute was too small, and the bottle of spirits broke, and in turn spoilt the packets of cigarettes. So much for the good intentions of the Sergeant's Mess!

Next, a farmer came over the brow to investigate the heap that had appeared on the hillside. Later in the day an RAF rescue party arrived and announced that they had parked the ambulance at least four miles away. A policeman then arrived from the other direction, from the east. Three of the crew were led down towards Bethesda, the body of the fourth being carried on a stretcher. They arrived at a large house in its own grounds and surrounded by trees. Here they were properly attended to, including Cooper with a broken nose. Later, it is sad to relate that Sergeant Stokes lost his life on 15th February 1944 in Lancaster ED841 of 166 Squadron flying from Kirmington, when it was shot down at Feldmark Freudenburg in Germany.

After a short sick-leave, Sergeant Cooper was posted to No 10 OTU at Harwell, and then to the Ferry Training Unit. In September 1942 he joined a crew to ferry a Wellington out to the Middle East, making initially for Gibraltar. A few nights later, they were preparing to take off, when one of the engines failed. In the morning a trail of oil was found all the way from dispersal to the end of the runway. On 3rd October they finally took off at night to fly the long route, not via Malta, to their destination. The route lay between the Canary Islands and the coast of Morocco. Suddenly the pilot, who was back at the Elsan at the time, shouted for the 2nd pilot to stop mucking about with the engines. The reply was that they were losing power in both engines, and the pilots turned the aircraft to port to head for the coast. All the spares and any loose equipment went out of the rear escape hatch to lighten the aircraft. It was soon evident that they would not make it though a lighthouse was spotted, so crash positions were taken. As soon as they hit the water, Cooper and the wireless operator exited from the astrodome, to find the dinghy already inflated with the rear gunner in it. The Wellington was going straight down. The pilot joined them from twenty feet below but the 2nd pilot, who had taken a crash position on the bed, never emerged.

Soon afterwards a Spanish fishing vessel picked them up, and they were given dry clothing. Thoughts of Gibraltar were rudely shattered when a Vichy French fighter appeared and sprayed bullets into the sea ahead of them. This was followed by the arrival of a Vichy French naval ship which took them off and deposited them in Agadir, where they were transferred at first to Rabat, then to a large prison compound at Laghouat as internees. Here washing facilities were limited, in horse troughs; both personal hygiene and washing clothes had to be carried out in rarely changed water. Apart from the size of the camp, it resembled the fort in the film *Beau Geste*. As solid food was scarce, the daily ration was two cups of red wine, two bowls of soup, and two slices of bread. The only food that was plentiful was dates, but these produced an unfortunate side effect, resulting in frequent visits to the lavatories.

These privations did not last too long, since the invasion of North Africa took place on 8th November 1942, and they were soon released, to be brought back to Greenock in one of the ships that had brought out the invasion force.

Sergeant Leslie Cooper, survivor from Anson N4980. *L Cooper*

Chapter Seven

A Halifax for Criccieth

(LL283)

Michael Kidston McGuire was born at Vernon, British Columbia in 1920. While he was studying at the University of British Columbia he joined the Canadian Officers Training Corps. In fact, not only was he an academic, but a great all rounder. He played cricket, rugby, badminton, hockey, tennis, was a fine horseman and went swimming and sailing.

When he applied at the recruiting office to join the RCAF as a pilot in April 1940 he was immediately snapped up as officer material, and was commissioned by December, at the same time as gaining his pilot's wings.

He became a flying instructor at No 9 SFTS at Trenton for a while, though he found time to court and marry Majorie Goodall in Montreal in June 1942. In December 1943 he was flown to England and eventually found himself at No 1664 Heavy Conversion Unit at Dishforth.

On the night of 30th August 1944, Flight Lieutenant McGuire took command of Halifax Mk.V serial LL283, for a cross country training flight. He noted several complaints on the acceptance Form 700 as to low oil pressure in the starboard inner engine, but these were within the prescribed limits, and his ground crew told him it would be OK.

The Halifax took off at 2050 hours with eight on board, being a normal crew plus a spare flight engineer, Sergeant A W Pack, gaining flight experience. All but the flight engineers were Canadians. Two hours into the flight, it was noticed that the oil pressure of the starboard inner engine had dropped to 40 pounds per square inch. Four and a half hours after take-off, the flight engineer notified the pilot that the reading was now zero, and unsuccessful attempts were made to feather the propeller. This was followed by the mid-upper gunner reporting that the engine was on fire. The captain warned the crew to prepare to abandon the aircraft.

At this time they were over the sea at 20,000 feet on a course of 190 degrees flying towards the bombing range on St Tudwal's Island off the Lleyn Peninsula. The navigator asked the captain to turn to head due east to ensure they would be over land. Shortly after this the order to bale out was given, and all the members of the crew jumped except for Sergeant Pack. The Halifax dived in flames and crashed into the side of a 580 feet hill near Ystum Gegid Isaf Farm, a few miles inland of Criccieth on Tremadoc Bay.

At 0150 hours Flight Lieutenant Tom Scudamore, medical officer and Mountain Rescue Team leader at RAF Llandwrog was notified by Flying Control of an aircraft crash near Portmadoc. He roused the team members and eventually reached the site of the Halifax scattered over three fields. On searching the wreckage the body of Sergeant Pack, the spare flight engineer, was found with an open parachute not fastened to his harness. It was later determined that the parachute was remote from him in the rest position and, although he reached it, once the aircraft went into a dive it was impossible to bale out. On contacting Llandwrog, Scudamore was informed that two members of the crew had been taken to the Portmadoc casualty reception station, having come down at Tremadoc and Criccieth. On reaching Portmadoc CRS, the medical officer found Sergeant J F Morris, air gunner in bed with head injuries, and an uninjured Sergeant M J Swan, who informed him that the other air gunner, Sergeant R S Lowe was seen to bale out.

At 0830 hours a message was received to say that an airman had arrived at a farm called Tyddyn Mawr in Cwm Ystradllyn, to the north. The MO and Flight Sergeant Murphy raced up to the farm set in a delightful valley, where they found Warrant Officer C J Hogan, the wireless operator. He had a sprained ankle and was suffering from shock, so a morphine injection was given on returning to Portmadoc. In the meantime another airman, Flight Sergeant R S Lowe had been brought in to the CRS with leg and buttock injuries. At 1000 hours a telephone message advised that two more crew members had walked down the mountains in Cwm Pennant to the farm of Braich Dinas to the north-west. On reaching them in an Army ambulance, the medical officer found Flying Officer H W W Bucke, bomb aimer, with a slight leg injury and Sergeant J D Abson with abrasions of the abdominal area. Otherwise they were in high spirits to have survived baling out in complete darkness.

Flight Lieutenant Scudamore realised that there was now only the pilot not accounted for and requested a search aircraft from Llandwrog. Eventually, after skilful low flying over the area the pilot spotted a parachute with a body high on Moel Ddu and dropped a flare to mark the spot. The body of Flight Lieutenant McGuire was recovered via Ynys Wen and Cwm Ystradllyn. He was unfortunate enough in all this wilderness to strike a wall with his head on landing and was killed outright.

The court of inquiry showed that the engine failure was due to bearing failure due to low oil pressure. This had been low since an engine overhaul and the bearings were worn and loose. Furthermore, the inability to feather the engine was because the big end bearing failure caused a connecting rod to break and puncture the cylinder and cut the feathering line. The outcome was to amend Merlin engine performance to allow a minimum oil pressure of 60 lbs/sq inch, not the 45 lbs which led to the failure of the engine in this aircraft.

On rejoining his Conversion Unit at Dishforth, Warrant Officer Hogan set off in Halifax JP204 on a cross-country training flight on 2nd October. It developed an engine fire and struck the ground near Galphay, Ripon. Three crew members baled out but the remaining five airmen, including W/O Hogan lost their lives.

A Halifax MkII with Merlin engines, similar to LL283 (MkV). *Harry Holmes*

Michael Kidston McGuire, later Flight Lieutenant and pilot of Halifax LL283. *Charles Birch*

Chapter Eight

The Lost Oxford of 418 Squadron (LB537)

By October 1944, airfields in France were back in Allied hands. Many fighter squadrons had transferred to them, and others with any excuse were flying in to snap up some of the French wines. The aircrews of 418 (RCAF) squadron were organising a party so they held a cash collection and sent over their communications aircraft, Airspeed Oxford LB537, flown by Hank Loriaux and navigated by Bill Sewell to St Dizier, east of Paris. This airfield, recently vacated by the Luftwaffe, was now occupied by the USAAF. On landing, the pair were taken to the Bar Officer, a red-haired Texan, in the wine cellar. He was surrounded by cases of Dom Perignon, the best cognac, champagne, and loads of wine from vineyards, where, it was claimed, French soldiers had to salute as they passed by. Hank and Bill were weathered in for three days while the Americans fed them on steak, apple pie and ice cream, washed down by the finest wines. When they finally took off, with more alcohol on board than in the tanks, they had to fly home to Hunsdon by map reading since the Oxford was not fitted with a radio or any navigational aids. On reaching the airfield they saw red Verey flares and were frantically directed to their relief airfield, where the contraband was swiftly removed. A customs officer had been at their base checking on rumours of illicit drinks being brought over. Hank and Bill went to their hut to shave and clean up. By the time they got to the party all that was left for them was a glass of champagne each!

On 5th January 1945 navigator George Drew and his pilot Tommy Matthew carried out a ground attack on German troop and vehicle movements around St Vith and Prum during the 'Battle of the Bulge' in their Mos-

quito Mk.IV. As a result of the cockpit heating failing they both caught colds, with Tommy being hospitalised. This meant that they could not go on leave until he recovered. Matthews was anxious to visit Paisley, where his wife Margaret had just arrived from Canada. He had not seen her for over a year.

A week later on 13th January 1945, George Drew booked Oxford LB537 for a flight to Abbotsinch, via Woodvale in Lancashire for refuelling. Warrant Officer Jim Firth was to be the pilot, and Drew to be the navigator. On hearing of this flight, Flying Officers Geoffrey (Happy) Day and Wal Retzer, asked to go along. However, on checking the weather forecast, Drew found 9/10ths low level cloud to Lancashire and thickening to Scotland. As the aircraft had no radio to obtain bearings, essential in those conditions, the flight was cancelled. Matthews appeared reconciled to a tedious train journey, so Drew set off to London on his motorcycle on leave. The next day the squadron adjutant telephoned Drew to tell him that the Oxford had taken off after all, but had not arrived at Woodvale. Air searches were instigated, but nothing was found.

Three weeks later, on 6th February, Owen Thomas, of Cornel Farm alongside Llyn Crafnant, was climbing the ridge towards Llyn Cowlyd to check on a flock of sheep he was holding for an auctioneer. A sudden thunderstorm forced him to take shelter under an overhanging rock. As he looked back towards his farm he saw on the skyline high above what appeared to be an aircraft. Returning to the farm he sent his daughter Dilys on her bicycle to raise the alarm at Trefriw police station. On reaching the crash site with Constable Griffiths they found the bodies of three airmen together resting against the rocks of locally named Cornel mountain. The RAF Mountain Rescue Team at RAF Llandwrog was notified at 1645 hours, arriving at the site by 2000 hours where the fourth member of the crew, Flight Lieutenant Matthews, was found some distance ahead of the Oxford. It was so late that the recovery of the bodies was left until the following day. On returning, the team members were distressed to find that in the meantime the airmen's bodies had been rifled and personal effects such as watches stolen, and even a flying helmet from an airman with serious head injuries.

Flight Lieutenant Tommy C Matthew.
Mrs Dilys Morris

Crews of 418 Squadron prepare for battle including, at the back 3rd from left F/O Wal Retzer, and from right 4th F/Lt Tommy Matthew with 5th his navigator F/O George Drew. *Public Archives of Canada*

George Drew became a passive survivor, but he lost a comrade who had shared 30 operational flights with him. Yearning for his wife cost Matthews his life and that of three of his friends. How the Oxford came to be 50 miles west of its intended course will never be known. Strangely, in the final moments of flight it appears to have been flying from the south-west, not south-east. The rocky summit it struck was at an altitude of only 1,300 feet. The investigation concluded that while W/O Firth had many flying hours as a pilot to his credit, he was not a skilled navigator. Also the flight, in an aircraft lacking radio and navigational aids, should not have been allowed.

For many years after this unfortunate event, Mr Thomas climbed up from his farm at Christmas to a hollybush which grew just below the crash site. He would cut berried holly sprigs and send them to the parents of Tommy Matthews in Glasgow, and of Geoffrey Day in Manchester.

Warrant Officer James Firth, pilot of Oxford LB537. *National Archives of Canada*

Sergeant, later Flying Officer, Geoffrey (Happy) Day. *Mrs Dilys Morris*

The splendid Mosquito memorial at Bradwell Bay, former home of 418 Squadron. The inscription reads:
RAF Bradwell Bay.
1942 - 1945
This memorial has been erected in memory of the 121 members of the allied air forces who in answer to the call of duty left the airfield to fly into the blue forever.
David Thorpe

Hill walker Ron Waldron inspects the wreckage from Oxford LB537 above Llyn Crafnant. Heather flowers bloom in memory of the crew in autumn.

Chapter Nine

Sixteen Gates
(Master AZ714)

The area to the north-east of Dolgellau, bounded by the valleys of the Afon Mawddach and Afon Wnion is dominated by 2408 feet Rhobell Fawr. It is a lonely, set back mountain, with little sign of the hand of man, apart from a narrow track meandering up to it.

On 11th July 1943, Sergeant Eric Galloway took off from Calveley airfield in Cheshire, on a routine training flight in Miles Master AZ714 of 17(P)Advanced Flying Unit. Soon visibility became poor with persistent rain and low cloud. After flying for an hour and a half he was forced to gingerly let down through the cloud with a hope of finding his bearings beneath it. Suddenly a rocky prominence loomed up and, although he tugged hard on the joystick, the Master clipped the top of the rocks and fell inverted onto a broad ledge.

On recovering, Galloway – surprised to find that he was still alive, made haste to extricate himself from the wreckage in case of fire. Not only was this extremely difficult from underneath the wreck, but he was suffering from a fractured ankle, head injuries, severe bruising and shock. Eventually he succeeded and started crawling away. He had to move sideways at first keeping away from the edge of the cliffs which rose in a series of ledges. The ground was rough with rocky outcrops which cradled spongy bogs fed now by the heavy rain. In time though he came to the end of the ledges where the southern area of the summit drained to a stream. Galloway followed this down through a difficult line of broken rocks, past a steep waterfall, and to the bottom of the cliffs. By extreme good fortune he found a ruined sheepfold, which would afford some little protection from the weather, and he

collapsed into it. He had crashed at 1230 hours; now it was almost evening, and he could move no further. At Calveley, Sergeant Galloway was posted as missing, and a telegram to his parents was initiated by the Air Ministry.

The next day as the rain relented, Evan Lloyd Davies, his son Lloyd Foster, and another farmer came onto the mountain. They rounded up one flock of sheep from the rocky part known as Ty Hir, and took them to the banks of a minor river, a tributary of the Afon Melau. Here they washed the sheep and dipped the lambs. On the way they were observed by Galloway. He called to them, but his weak voice was drowned by the bleating of the animals. He lapsed into a state of depression and waited to die.

However, the entourage returned with Lloyd Davies arriving first to open a gate nearby for the sheep. Galloway shouted with all his might just one last time before the sheep arrived. Just opposite the waterfall Mr Davies became aware of a faint cry. He headed up into the rocks where he found the injured airman, now suffering from acute exposure. He called up the others as they came through the gate, and Evan Davies, who had a regular job as a signalman, took off his heavy railway coat and placed it over Galloway.

Lloyd Davies then set off across the wet and boggy land in a direct line to Blaenau Hall where he raised the alarm. Soon the casualty was evacuated with the help of police and an ambulance which was driven with great difficulty along the miles from the main road near Rhydymain to the sheep-wash. In all the crew had to open and close sixteen gates in each direction!

Sergeant Galloway made a complete recovery, though it took eight months before he resumed flying in Northumberland, far away from the Welsh mountains.

Sergeant E L Galloway, pilot of Master AZ714. *Mrs Pamela King (sister)*

Rescuer Lloyd Foster Davies opens one of the sixteen gates. *Mary Doylerush*

Presumed crash site of Master AZ714 on lonely Rhobell Fawr. *Author*

Photographs on the following page:

Miles Master I. *Chaz Bowyer*

Cindy investigates the ruined sheepfold where Sergeant Galloway was found. *Author*

Chapter Ten

The Firefly (WJ153)
and The Moth (N6933)

The following three chapters are associated with RAF Llanbedr, so a short introduction is included. This airfield opened in June 1941 accommodating fighter squadrons for the defence of Liverpool and coastal shipping, controlled by RAF Valley. Later, its main role was as an Armament Practice Camp, where successive RAF and USAAF fighter squadrons flew in to practice gunnery skills by shooting up targets on the beach, or at target drogues trailed behind Henleys, Lysanders, and Martinets, aircraft supplied by RAF Towyn – as observed by the author as an ATC cadet at my first camp at Llanbedr in July 1943. Post war there was a transition to use by the Royal Aircraft Establishment to provide aircraft for the Aberporth firing range over Cardigan Bay. The current operator is FRASerco, operating on a ten year contract from the Defence Evaluation and Research Agency.

The Firefly

Fairey Firefly (military serial number WJ153) took off on a test flight on 22nd April 1954 from the Royal Aircraft Establishment unit based at Llanbedr. The pilot was Flight Lieutenant 'Dicky' Dickinson RAFVR, and the observer Junior Technician Alan Hawkins, RAF. The Llanbedr Fireflies had two roles; many – brightly coloured red and yellow, were used as targets by the guided missile unit at Aberporth, and were pilotless radio-controlled aircraft. They were radar targets, not meant to be actually shot down! Ground staff controlled the aircraft on take-off and landing, then a crewed Firefly took over and flew with them as lookout shepherds and controllers in the air on the flight to and from the range over Cardigan Bay. Firefly WJ153 was one of these.

The flight was the second of the day to resolve some problems experienced earlier. They had climbed to the ceiling of the Firefly at 25,000 feet when engine power suddenly reduced alarmingly. The aircraft was over the sea to the north of the Lleyn peninsula so, after checking on his position, the pilot notified base of this and his intention to ditch. Hawkins had an immediate problem because the dinghy, which should have been on the parachute, had been dropped loose into the seat pan since it was difficult to enter with the combined weight of parachute and dinghy. As he made hasty notes on this more than usually interesting flight, he was attempting to fasten the dinghy so that it would leave the aircraft with him.

In the meantime the pilot, by using booster and priming pumps, managed to restart the engine, and notified base that he would set course for Llanbedr. Soon after this, the engine lost power again at around 4,000 feet, though by now they were over land and sinking fast. The point of no return for baling out was passed and they would have to attempt a landing. Hawkins tightened his seat harness. Dickinson lowered the landing gear using the accumulator back-up system and headed for a convenient flat-looking field. With a dead engine the aircraft was aerodynamically more like a flying brick, so Dickinson quickly selected landing flap to help the landing attitude.

Hawkins recalls 'The next few seconds extended into minutes. I saw the wingtips hit the ground. Things went brown, possibly due to dust clouds, or more likely the g forces on the brain. There were three distinct and violent impacts, and I kept thinking when is this b— thing going to stop rolling. When we eventually came to rest in a hedge we were upright and still alive. It seemed to take a long time to release the seat and parachute harness and climb out onto the remains of the port mainplane. Dicky was muttering about mag switches to Off and Ground Flight switch to Ground. I said the word 'Out' to him and lifted him upright and almost out of the cockpit. He was a well-built chap I could not have lifted normally so the adrenaline must have been working overtime. We stood watching petrol running over the engine when the first civilian arrived, followed by a field full of spectators, police, and disappointed fire and ambulancemen'.

The Firefly had crashed near the farmstead of Pen-y-bythod, about a mile southwest of the village of Llandwrog. Mr Richard Williams, of the farm was the first on the scene. After being given tea and cakes at the farm, the two crew were transported to RAF Llandwrog where the MO pronounced them officially alive and found that they had suffered mainly minor injuries including severe bruising. While the precise reason for the crash was not found, failure of the throttle linkage was suggested.

For Alan Hawkins, a collision in his car with a stone wall some years later seemed quite mild compared with this incident.

The Moth

Another incident associated with Llanbedr had occurred a few years earlier. On 7th May 1948 two members of No 25 RFS flew to Llanbedr in de Havilland Tiger Moth N6933 to make arrangements for summer camp for the University Air Squadrons later that year. After lunch in the Sergeants Mess the Moth took off and headed south, but soon afterwards collided with the mountain slope which rises from the shore near Llwyngwril. Both airmen survived, but the aircraft was a complete write-off except for the engine, which was recovered, and then the remains set on fire.

The Moth had been refuelled and preflight checks carried out by Ted Cross and Colin Sell of the Llanbedr Instrument Section. Colin Sell was also a Target Towing Operator and in June 1949 survived a forced landing in a Miles Martinet which suffered

RAF Observer Alan Hawkins. *A Hawkins*

Firefly WM859, pilot J Sharman, January 1955 at Llanbedr. *Ted Cross*

Firefly WJ153 forced landing near Llandwrog in 1954. *Alan Hawkins*

engine failure, coming down on the anti-aircraft gun emplacement area at Tonfanau. On 29th July he was flying in another Martinet to take part in an Army exercise at Tonfanau target range when again engine failure was experienced. Pilot I P J Evans, made a successful ditching in heavy seas, and both airmen were able to get clear of the aircraft before it sank off Barmouth. Sell threw out the dinghy but, due to inexperience, cut the tie before the dinghy inflated with the result that it went straight down. Although the lifeboat made a speedy appearance to pick them up, LAC Colin Sell was drowned, but the pilot was saved.

Tiger Moth N6933 at Llanbedr. AM 7th May 1948. *Ted Cross*

Tiger Moth N6933 near Llywngwril. PM 7th May 1948. *Ted Cross*

F/Lt 'Dickie' Dickinson, pilot of Firefly WJ153. *Barn Smith*

Spitfire TE435 from Llanbedr suffered engine failure on 24th November 1948, force landing on the beach near Harlech. The pilot survived. *Ted Cross*

Chapter Eleven

Wellingtons at Llanbedr
(N2866 and HE872)

The Battle of Heligoland Bight and Beyond
Early in the war Bomber Command were forbidden to attack targets on land in Germany for fear of the whole might of the Luftwaffe being turned against an unready Britain and a France with few modern aircraft to defend their cities. Therefore attacks were carried out against naval ships on 14th December 1939 by the best bomber of the time – Vickers Wellingtons. Even so, five Wellingtons of No 99 squadron were lost. On 18th December a large force (for the time) of 24 Wellingtons from Nos 9, 37, and 149 Squadrons was mustered for an attack on shipping at Wilhelmshaven, with the constraint that no land targets or shipping at the dockside could be hit for fear of killing civilians.

On arrival at Wilhelmshaven the force was met by intense flak including that from the battleships *Scharnhorst* and *Gneisenau*. Like all the other battleships they were neatly tied up at the dockside and could not be touched! Four merchantmen in the centre of the harbour became their only targets, but the price for the few bombs that were dropped on them was impossibly high. Out of the 22 Wellingtons which arrived in the area, only seven survived flak and attacks from a large force of Messerschmitt Me109s and 110s to fight again. Ten were shot down, two ditched on their way home, and three were written off when they crash landed back in England. The Luftwaffe lost two Me 109s. Following this action, where this type of daylight operation was seen not to be justified, Bomber Command would switch its operations to the cloak of night where the crews would stand some chance.

Of the survivors one was Wellington N2980 of No 149 squadron, which later went to 20 OTU at Lossiemouth in October 1940. On 31st December, on a flight over Scotland, engine failure forced the captain to ditch in Loch Ness. In 1976 American researchers, using sonar equipment to search for Nessie, located the Wellington on the lake bed. 'R for Robert' was successfully recovered in September 1985 and painstakingly renovated and placed on display at her birthplace, now Brooklands Museum at Weybridge.

Another survivor from the 149 squadron attack was Wellington N2866, piloted by Flying Officer Riddlesworth. This aircraft eventually found its way to 18 OTU at Hucknall. On 15th October 1941, N2866 was on a cross country training flight when it suffered engine failure due to icing. Later there was an engine fire which the pilot dealt with successfully. Pilot Officer Mendela managed to make a forced landing on a hillside just east of RAF Llanbedr. All eight of the mainly Polish crew survived without serious injury. The rear gunner, A/C Jenkins who was Welsh, was glad to be back in his homeland and headed for the nearest farmhouse at Llwynion, where he had a great welcome and was given a nice cup of tea.

Wellington HE872
On 25th September 1943, air bomber Sergeant Harry George arrived at RAF Wing, the home of 26 Operational Training Unit. Here he was crewed up with pilot Sergeant Les Edwards of Conway, navigator Flight Sergeant John Chigwidden RAAF, wireless operator J C Watts RAAF, and Sergeants Hupage and M O'Hanlon, the air gunners.

On 3rd November they took off in Wellington HE872 for a last cross country training flight before going to a conversion unit for four-engined bombers. As Sergeant George was also the front turret gunner, he fired 600 rounds ammunition at a firing range before the Wellington climbed to 16,000 feet. Suddenly they entered dark cumulo-nimbus cloud, and everything went haywire. 'I was pinned to the roof of the aircraft by the forces that took control of us and then the aircraft started a steep dive. The dive was so steep that anything loose hurtled towards the nose. Throughout this disconcerting episode there was the terrific noise of the engines as we careered downwards in cloud. Les and I were pulling back on the stick to no avail, but eventually the rate of descent eased off. Les could not maintain height and we were still going down but we were happier as we now had more control. We broke cloud over water with the plane still refusing to maintain height. We were so relieved to survive the dive that we said 'Ditch it Les', but then like the end of a bad dream a runway appeared ahead. Still descending and lined up perfectly, Edwards landed at Llanbedr aerodrome'.

Next day, after the mechanics had worked on the Wellington, George and Chiggwidden asked the pilot if they might go into the village while an air test was carried out, which was agreed. However, on return they heard the disturbing news that their aircraft had crashed. The flight was to have been with the remaining four crew and two others. In fact the aircraft gathered speed along the runway, but never achieved take-off. It careered into outbuildings at Ynys Farm.

Sergeant Hupage, the mid-upper gunner was killed, along with an electrician, LAC I W Jones. The rear gunner, Sergeant M O'Hanlon suffered head injuries and had appalling headaches afterwards. The subsequent inquiry found that the aircraft trim had been too far forward, and put it down to the inexperience of the captain.

Following hospital treatment, Sergeant Edwards did not have the strength to handle a heavy bomber, because of arm injuries; and so the remaining crew were split up. Harry George went to No.115 (Lancaster) Squadron and survived a tour of operations. Their Lancaster, KO-K, went missing soon afterwards. John Chigwidden went to 622 Squadron on Lancasters. They were on a mission to Homberg on 21st July 1944, when their aircraft GI-Q was shot down. All the crew lost their lives, and are buried at Tilberg in the Netherlands. 'Chig', as his friends called him, was on his 13th mission.

The other Wellington crew member not on the test flight, Flight Sergeant J J Chigwidden. *H George*

Photographs on the following page:

Wellington Mk1c N2980 R-Robert (sister aircraft of N2866) lovingly restored at Brooklands Museum. Propellers are bent back from ditching on Loch Ness in 1940. *Brooklands Museum Trust Ltd/Cliff Knox via Wendy Thomas*

Harry George, far left, not aboard his Wellington HE872 when it crashed on a test flight at Llanbedr. *H George*

Chapter Twelve

The Hunted Ones

The title refers to the Jindivik, an Aboriginal word which gives its name to the joint Australian/British pilotless aircraft. These gradually replaced radio controlled Fireflies and Meteors at Llanbedr in the 1960s. The Jindiviks are accompanied now by a Hawk as a shepherd acting as 'eyes', or a Hunter when the Hawk is in maintenance. On reaching the range, an area of Cardigan Bay controlled by Aberporth, a decoy target is released by a winch and flown behind the Jindivik. This consists of a streamlined metal container with fins which carries infra-red (for Sidewinder) or semi-active radar (for Skyflash) sources. The Jindivik is controlled and manoeuvred for the entire flight by a team of ground controllers at Llanbedr. Strict control is kept on the operation of the Jindiviks, and only four have managed to 'escape' in flight over land in all the years of these operations. We may view this in the perspective that the 7,000th launch of the Jindiviks will take place early in 1999. This is the story of the four escapers.

24th June 1963. Jindivik Mk102B A92-248 suffered an autopilot malfunction following an overshoot. It then headed north from Llanbedr and crashed three miles north of Porthmadoc.

27th September 1966. During a family holiday in North Wales, a Norwich family were returning to Prenteg near Porthmadoc along the B4391 Bala to Ffestiniog road. Mr Thomas Robinson, a retired policeman was driving, accompanied by his wife Harriet, and their son David and his wife, who was expecting a baby. Suddenly, Mr Robinson heard the ever increasing sound of an aircraft engine coming towards them. Out of the blue a Jindivik aircraft skimmed over a stone wall, bounced on the roof of the car, and crashed into the hillside beyond where it burst into flames at Pont Afon Gan. Mr Robinson stopped the car and, after checking that none of his family were hurt, rushed up the slope to see if he could help the pilot, not knowing that it carried none.

However, he was driven back by several explosions caused by the fire, and awaited the rescue services. He was greatly relieved to find that it was a pilotless aircraft (Jindivik A92-448 Mk103A). Amazingly, neither he nor any member of his family had been injured, and were suffering only from shock.

29th July 1983. Jindivik A92-715 (Mk103A) crashed into sand dunes near Llanbedr on final approach. The electronics were presumed to have been affected by a bird strike, and modifications were then made to prevent a repetition.

14th May 1991. Leslie Cox and his wife Betty were taking an early holiday in north west Wales at a caravan park at Dyffryn Ardudwy. On this day they drove to the nearby sand dunes and sat in their Ford Sierra, relaxing and taking in the sun, facing the sea. At 1539 hours a Jindivik had begun its landing approach on runway 36 accompanied by a Hawk shepherd, after a sortie to the Aberporth range.

Leslie Cox: 'It was a very quiet and peaceful evening, we were enjoying the tranquillity. To the right, a few hundred yards away, was the landing strip of Llanbedr airbase. To our left we heard the sound of aircraft, we looked in that direction and saw two aircraft flying towards us, they were flying very low. One was a Jindivik with its minder and was losing height. About a hundred yards from us it struck the top of a tree and skidded along the ground and burst into flames. It was heading straight towards our car. I was sitting in the front of the car, my wife in the rear. I shouted to her "Bet, in a few seconds from now we will be incinerated" – she replied "Les we've had it!".

'As the plane neared the car it lifted slightly; the fuselage went across the bonnet in front of me. The wing went over the car roof, but the undercarriage smashed into the engine with a terrific bang and flames enveloped the car, I sat for a moment dazed, surprised that we were still in one piece. I managed to open the twisted door, and ran from the car, my wife doing the same. We stood there in a daze, I couldn't see. I thought I was blind, but when I wiped my eyes it was blood covering the lens of my glasses – some glass had cut into my scalp.

'As we stood there we heard sirens and soon an ambulance and fire tender were approaching.' Betty Cox ran towards the plane hoping to help the pilot inside, not knowing there was none. Then someone came along and turned her back.

Leslie Cox: 'An angel in the form of nurse Alice Ash came to our assistance and steered us into the ambulance where we were whisked to the first aid unit at the airfield. She was so kind, she hugged us, loved us, and was very consoling. While waiting for the doctor she phoned our relatives to assure them we were safe before the news media and television reported the accident.

'Later we were transported to a four star hotel and given the honeymoon suite.' A fitting reward for unlikely survivors.

The escapee culprit was Jindivik Mk.103B A92-706 . Each incident was followed by a meticulous investigation. In this case the lesson learned was to have the shepherd aircraft follow the Jindivik up to the runway threshold, where any deviation from the normal would be spotted immediately, and appropriate action taken.

Jindivik at the moment of leaving its trolley at Llanbedr. Diffwys in the Rhinog range beyond. *MoD*

Jindivik with Meteor shepherd over Cardigan Bay. *MoD*

Aftermath of the Jindivik crash. The car occupants were lucky to be alive. *Timothy Ferris*

Chapter Thirteen

Peril in Padarn

(Wessex XR524)

While researching for a 50th anniversary memorial article on the mainly wartime losses of Air Training Corps cadets, published in the *Air Cadet Review* of August 1992, the writer came across many sad stories. One of these concerned three cadets of the Chapel-en-le-Frith Flight of 1180 (Buxton) Squadron, who lost their lives in Lancaster JB153 of No 103 Squadron, Elsham Wolds, which crashed on a cross-country training flight near Wymeswold airfield on 8th September 1943. The crew of six and the cadets stood no chance, theirs being the highest loss of cadets in one aircraft. I was able to obtain photographs of the cadets, their characters shining forth. I never again expected to feel a loss so keenly for cadets I had not known, modern military aircraft being so much safer. A few days before this loss, as a cadet in the Colwyn Bay County School (1533) Flight, I was told that two cadets of our town Squadron, No 271, had lost their lives when Anson EG278 disintegrated over farmland near Caernarfon on the 4th September. On the very day of the Lancaster crash I was in the guard of honour at the funeral service for the Colwyn Bay cadets, doing my duty and pondering about fate.

Close on fifty years later, in August 1993, cadets of the East Lancashire Wing of the Air Training Corps were at RAF Valley for their summer camp. This is a week each year greatly anticipated by cadets, almost as good as being in the service for them; such a lot to observe, and learn, and so importantly, a chance to fly. That is what it is all about.

On Thursday 12th August four cadets were given the opportunity of a training flight in Westland Wessex XR524 of C Flight, No 22 Search and Rescue Squadron. They were 15 year old Cadet Christopher Bailey whose ambition was to be a Tornado pilot; he had already flown for the first time there in a Chipmunk, and had only joined 1471 (Horwich) Sqn three months earlier, 16 year old Cadet Cpl Sarah Coker of 1036 (Bury) Sqn, 16 year old Cadet Mark Oakden, also of 1036 Sqn, who wanted to become a pilot, and 17 year old Cadet Sgt Amanda Whitehead, also of 1036 and a good friend of Sarah Coker. Amanda had joined five years earlier and had been a founder member of the squadron band.

All of them dreamed of joining the RAF one day. After some instruction, the Wessex took off after lunch with the four cadets, the pilot and navigator, and a winchman in the main cabin with the cadets. Some 25 minutes later, on reaching Llyn Padarn near Llanberis there was a loud ominous bang from the rear of the Wessex. In fact the drive shaft to the tail rotor had snapped. With no directional control the helicopter spun down towards the lake like a sycamore leaf. The pilot, Flight Lieutenant Keith Macguire, fought to at least keep it level. The winchman, Flight Lieutenant Paul Todd, hurriedly strapped himself in. Fifteen seconds later the Wessex hit the surface of the lake. While not quite as hard as a land impact would have been, it was still severe.

Cadet Coker: 'I tried to get the seatbelt off, but I was pulling it the wrong way. I had to tell myself to calm down and remember the right things to do. I managed to get it off in the end but by this time there was all this icy black water gushing in through the door. I didn't even have time to take a breath of air. I couldn't see anything and couldn't breathe. I remember feeling around for the door and

The last moments of Wessex XR524 as it hits the surface of Llyn Padarn. *North Wales Weekly News*

not being able to find it. But somehow I got out and inflated my lifejacket.

There was no chance to see what had happened to any of the others. I wasn't in any pain then. I remember rising to the surface. The water around me was going from black to grey and then I broke the surface.'

A warden of Parc Padarn, Paula Roberts, was in a boat nearby and headed for the scene with two canoeists who jumped aboard. There was no sign of the helicopter: it had sunk almost immediately. However the three crew had got out and shouted that there were four others to account for. Suddenly they spotted Sarah Coker and sped over, lifted her into the boat and headed for the shore. Sarah had suffered spinal injuries and was transferred to hospital by ambulance. The three crewmen were taken in another Wessex which had been on a exercise nearby.

The bodies of the other cadets were recovered later; all had drowned. The speed at which the crash occurred in unfamiliar surroundings gave them little chance of survival. Cadet Coker was very fortunate to find the doorway and keep calm in those traumatic moments. The RAF Board of Inquiry found that the problem centred on the design of the Wessex, which allows the tail section to be folded back on itself to reduce parking space. In this case the coupling was not fully engaged when the tail section was put together with the body, but allowed the aircraft to take off. The coupling came apart in flight and, when it tried to re-engage, the load was so great that the shaft failed.

As a former cadet the writer felt these losses, with the cadets photographs from their parents in my hand, most keenly.

Amanda, Christopher, and Mark, your memory lives on.

Wessex XR524 being recovered. The door from which Cadet Sarah Coker escaped can be seen. *North Wales Weekly News*

Wessex XR524 tail section being recovered. *North Wales Weekly News*

Cadet Amanda Whitehead.
*Whitehead family
via East Lancs ATC*

Cadet Mark Oakden.
*Oakden family
via East Lancs ATC*

Cadet Christopher Bailey.
*Bailey family
via East Lancs ATC*

Cadet Sarah Coker.
North Wales Weekly News

**The author's
granddaughter Laura
peruses the bilingual ATC
memorial on Llyn Padarn
lakeside.** *Author*

Chapter Fourteen

Through the Looking Glass
(Botha W5142)

Looking across the Menai Strait from Beaumaris, at the nearest mountain, Moel Wnion (Onion Hill), one can see a scar in the grass near the summit. This story is about how the scar came about.

Squires Gate airfield, on the outskirts of Blackpool, was for several wartime years the base of No 3 School of General Reconnaissance. Here observers practised gaining skills in cross-country navigation. For part of the course trainees were given about six locations to find, photograph, and write reports on. These included Stranraer harbour, a butter factory on Anglesey, and Telford's bridge over the Menai Strait.

On 20th July 1942 Blackburn Botha W5142 took off, with Flight Sergeant J M Foster at the controls, to find a road and railway crossover on the north Wales coast near the village of Aber. On board was Flight Sergeant L Moss, the wireless operator, and three Sergeant observers, L H Ganner, J Haig, and J A Rawlinson; also a young medical orderly who had come along for a joyride. There would not be much joy on this trip.

After a sea crossing they banked over Bangor, turning east along the coast. There was a bank of cloud hugging the hills, but the sea and coastal strip was clear. Haig was carrying out the navigation and soon found the location. Rawlinson was charged with taking the photographs with a big lens, trigger operated RAF P51 camera, and writing the report. He had to hang the heavy camera out of the starboard window, but just as he had the subject in the viewfinder, some trees intervened. He asked the pilot to turn round so that he could try again. Unfortunately, instead of turning over the sea, Foster elected to turn to starboard into the cloud. Rawlinson hung onto the camera, waiting for the bridge to reappear in his viewfinder.

Suddenly he found grass flashing by under the nose of the aircraft. The pilot was heaving back and back on the control column to get the nose up. However, the Botha collided with the top of the mountain. Just a few feet more and they would have made it. When Rawlinson came round, he found himself on the floor with a terrible headache and a pain in his backside. The pilot was hanging forward, supported by his seat straps, in a very dazed condition. A strong smell of petrol permeated everywhere, and terrified sheep were bleating incessantly.

It was nearly an hour after the crash before the crew started to pull themselves together. All had survived, though badly knocked about and suffering from shock. The medical orderly had vanished, hopefully to find help. The Botha was an absolute wreck, with both engines ripped out. There was a terrible gash in the hillside made by the port wing and fuselage. After studying the maps the survivors staggered down the steep slope, in the general direction of the sea. Some hundred yards later, they encountered some farm labourers looming up out of the mist, with pitchforks at the ready. With a lack of English on the one hand, and a lack of Welsh on the other, it was some time before the fact that they were British airmen was established. Following the crash of an enemy bomber nearby the previous year, the local populace were understandably a little edgy.

The crew were guided down to a track towards Aber, passing on the way one of the Botha's engines which had rolled down to a wall. They walked in a line though the village, causing a lot of interest in their dishevelled state, and the fact that Rawlinson's injury to his bottom meant that he walked along unaware that the seat of his trousers was hanging down. They were invited into a farmhouse where the farmer's wife plied them with hot sweet tea, ideal for their state of shock, before they were whisked away to hospital in Bangor. The medical orderly, after raising the alarm vanished in the direction of his base. He was like the man who never was, not even appearing on the crash report. John Rawlinson was at the C&A Hospital, Bangor for some three weeks looked after by, among others, a tall, statuesque, gorgeous staff nurse by the name of Menna Evans. Months later he returned to Squires Gate to complete his course, and found to his surprise that the camera was recovered intact, and he had been awarded high marks for photographs taken up until the crash.

In February 1943 he crewed up with pilot Sergeant H Corbin during operational training at Catfoss in Yorkshire, then headed for the Overseas Aircraft Preparation Unit at Filton, near Bristol, where they took charge of a brand new Beaufighter. This was flown to No 304 Ferry Training Unit at Port Ellen, on the remote island of Islay. Here they flew out over the Atlantic, and back sometimes at night, in bitterly cold weather for the two week course which involved determining the exact fuel consumption of their aircraft, vital on overseas ferry flights.

In May the crew now received orders to join a squadron in the Middle East, so departed for Portreath in Cornwall to take on a full fuel load. Their initial destination, Ras-el-Mar, in Morocco, was at the limit of range for a Beaufighter. Halfway across the Bay of Biscay they sighted a Junkers Ju 88. Unfortunately, no guns had been fitted to their aircraft, the Brownings were actually lying loose on the floor! The pilot had no choice but to dive into a convenient layer of cloud, and they later emerged over the north-west corner of Spain.

The Moroccan coast was crossed on target, and they headed for the Sbu valley to take them to Fes. The pilot became lost at this point and Rawlinson went forward with the maps to check their position. At the same time they flew into thick cloud and a severe rainstorm, a situation not helped by the knowledge that there were high mountains to either side. Also there were still at least twenty miles to go, and the fuel gauges were showing empty. Then there was an almighty crash.

Hours later, Rawlinson awoke in a farmhouse, at El Menzel par Bir Tam Tam, with a badly injured leg. His pilot was alongside, with head injuries. Both were taken to Fes, and both survived. Avoiding the Junkers had used up precious fuel, so resulting in the crash. Sergeant Corbin recovered well enough to fly Mosquitos, but Sergeant Rawlinson was invalided out, his RAF career blighted by inclement weather and mountains. His navigator on the Botha flight, Johnny Haig, fared worse, believed shot down in a Beaufighter on an operational flight over the Bay of Biscay.

Sergeant John Rawlinson, survivor of Botha W5142 on Moel Wnion. *J Rawlinson*

Chapter Fifteen

At the Castle Gates
(Halifax HR723)

*The sight of a photograph of Conway Castle
will always produce a misty eye in Canadian
Jim Dunlop. It evokes the memory of a night in
1944 when he nearly drowned in its shadow.*

On 27th October 1944, Halifax HR723, code
QY-P, took off from Wombleton, Yorkshire,
base of 1666 Heavy Conversion unit, part of
No 6 (Canadian) Group, Bomber Command.
At the controls was Flight Lieutenant
Harold D O'Neil, of Calgary, with Flying
Officer Dunlop navigating, Flying Officer
W A Steele as bomb aimer, Pilot Officer
H W Ferris as wireless operator, and
Sergeant Jack Wagstaff as flight engineer.
The complement was made up by Sergeants
Mike Gurica, mid-upper gunner, and Norm
Miller rear gunner. Wagstaff was the only
RAF member in an otherwise Canadian
crew. Harry O'Neil, Jim Dunlop, and Hank
Ferris were good friends, having flown
together on Coastal Command and convoy
duties out of Newfoundland in Lockheed
Hudsons.

The route taken by the Halifax was base-
Reading-Bath, with a simulated bombing run
on an infra-red target. They then headed out
over the Bristol Channel and took a norther-
ly course, after which the the aircraft banked
north-easterly for Yorkshire. The flight then
became a severe trial for O'Neil: 'We had
been briefed to fly at 17,000 feet, which was
reached after engaging the superchargers,
but these did not seem to be functioning
properly. Plus two boost could only be maintained at full throttle and 2,500 rpm. We then
began to lose altitude and levelled out at
15,000 feet where we changed to 'M' gear. In
order to save fuel we descended again to
12,000 feet until forced higher by clouds (to

avoid icing up). 16,000 feet was reached and
the superchargers were tried again, to no
effect. Height was lost to 14,000 feet'

And so the battle of man versus machine
went on. To anyone able to view this aircraft
it would have appeared to be going up and
down like a yo-yo. The flight engineer would
also have been involved assisting the pilot.
O'Neil: 'Several alterations of course were
made to avoid cumulo-nimbus cloud. This
up and down process continued, each
descent resulting in more ice being accumu-
lated. At last we were unable to climb, and a
rapid descent started. All during the descent
ice was gathering, and despite efforts to
keep the controls free, they gradually
became jammed. I gave the order to put on
parachutes and be ready to bale out.'

At this point Dunlop advised him that they
were over the sea, and could they hold on
until they were over land? The H2S radar,
which was especially good at showing the
dividing line between land and sea, was
monitored. As soon as they crossed the coast
the pilot gave the order for the crew to bale
out, which they all acknowledged. The exit
for the navigator, bomb aimer, and wireless
operator was in the nose just aft of the bomb
sight. As Ferris was busy sending out the
SOS, Jim Dunlop reached round the curtain
partition to make sure he had on his chest
parachute pack. There was no panic, everyone calmly carried out the often practised
drill. The bomb aimer graciously stepped
back so that Dunlop was first out of the nose
hatch into the darkness. The mid-upper and
tail gunners left through the rear hatch.

On the ground, hundreds of people around
Llandudno Junction, and nearby coastal
towns came out to watch the drama unfold.

The pilot, before he left, set the aircraft on a course out to sea as best he could. However, it seemed like an unwanted dog which had latched onto them, and kept coming round. It was seen on its last wild foray to head over the Little Orme towards Colwyn Bay, then circle back for the last time over Llandudno's north shore. Dunlop saw the flash at 2335 hours as their aircraft hit the ground and hoped everyone had got out in time.

He then observed the River Conway coming up fast, and tried to steer clear, but with no lights to judge the drift he ended up in the cold water. Just before he hit he felt for the parachute release box, but the knob was missing, probably knocked off on the edge of the hatch. The Mae West, however, inflated immediately, and he was carried downriver by the outgoing tide. Much later he managed to unhook the parachute and, since no shoreline could be seen, started blowing his survival whistle. Finally he heard a man calling from the shore, and he swam towards the welcome voice in the wilderness, and the dim illumination from a cigarette lighter. It was Mr Richard Price, Head Gardener at Benarth, who arrived with Miss Hilda Wadle (now Mrs Roberts), a Land Army girl, at the water's edge, by the outlet of the Gyffin stream, close by Conway castle. He grabbed hold of the navigator, and pulled him onto rocks. Here Mr Price cut off the parachute harness, and carried Dunlop up to his house. His wet uniform was removed by Mr and Mrs Price, while young Miss Wadle was sent out of the room. He was then given a hot bath before being taken to Llandudno Junction Police Station.

When Bill Steele, the bomb aimer, pulled the ripcord his flying boots shot off as the parachute opened. Although he was fortunate to come down on mud flats on the east bank of the river, he had to plod through thick mud to Llandudno Junction railway station. His feet were so cold he practically put them right in the stove fire. Here he met Gurica who had come down in the same area. Millar and Wagstaff came down in fields near Hendre Wen Farm. The Canadian sprained an ankle on landing but was soon helped to the farm by Tom and Elizabeth Davies from Pabo Lane who had seen the descending parachutes. The pilot, last to leave the aircraft, broke cloud at about 1,000 feet and came down near Dinerth Road, Rhos-on-Sea. There was no sign of Hank Ferris.

Warrant Officer H 'Hank' W Ferris, killed in baling out of Halifax HR723. *National Archives of Canada*

Cigarette lighter made of aluminium from the Pedew Halifax by an Italian PoW. Mickey Mouse was just as popular then! *Glyn Davies*

The crew of Halifax HR723 reformed after the accident. Back L-R, F/Lt H D O'Neil, P/O W A Steele, Sgt J A Wagstaff, P/O B M Dunlop. Front L-R, Sgt McKay (replaced W/O Ferris), Sgt Gurica, Sgt J W Millar. *Jim Dunlop*

The next morning the body of the wireless operator was found in a field at what is now the Pinewood Riding Stables. He had not fastened the leg straps on his harness and, when his parachute opened, he fell straight through. He was buried in the military plot at Blacon Cemetery, Chester, where lie many of his Canadian comrades.

The rest of the crew returned to Wombleton, where they finished their course with a new wireless operator, Flying Officer McKay, who had completed a tour on Stirlings. They were then posted to No 429 Squadron at Leeming. It was the practise for incoming pilots to go on an operation with an experienced crew as a 'second dickie' pilot. Thus Flying Officer O'Neil duly went on his first mission on the night of 6/7th December 1944, and was reported missing with the whole crew. This was a great blow for his own crew who were moved around until they were given a new pilot, Flying Officer Martindale. They then completed seventeen operations before the war ended.

Halifax HR723 had crashed at Bodyscawen Farm, Bryn Pedew, the home of Mr and Mrs Zachariah Jones and their fifteen year old son, John Glyn, where it demolished outbuildings in the form of shippon, chaffing shed, and float shed. Though joined to the farmhouse, they were separated from it as if by a giant knife. The Halifax swept on through an orchard and a hedge before crossing the road and careering up a slope. Two cows, a pony, sow, and the flock of hens were killed. John Glyn's sixteen rabbits in a large hutch just vanished. Not even a scrap of

Halifax Mk.III HR723, which crashed at Pedew on 27th October 1944. It is seen here as LQ-N of 405 (Vancouver) Squadron at Gransden Lodge, Bedfordshire, on 10th August 1943. *National Archives of Canada*

fur was ever found. Strangely, before the aircraft crashed, Mrs Jones was prompted to look out of the bedroom window where she saw the haystack on fire some twenty-five yards away. Down below, Pero the sheepdog, who had been locked in one of the outhouses, was barking furiously. Two hens were seen near him in the light of the fire and they survived, presumably until Christmas. How had they and the dog got out before the crash? Pero disappeared in all this mayhem but came back, singed, several days later. Zachariah Jones was never the same after all that trauma.

Hundreds of people, including the writer, visited the site next morning. It was like a car boot sale on a gigantic scale with all sorts of goodies on display, a dinghy, instruments, miles of brightly colour-coded wire, a flying helmet. But not for long. Anything portable just melted away. We were gladdened to know that no-one had been killed there.

The crash itself produced a strange consequence. At the meeting of the Water and Gas Committee of Llandudno UDC in May 1945, the members had to consider reducing the water charge to Bodysgawen Farm 'because of loss of supply due to an aeroplane crash'. The Committee reduced the charge from 19/3d to 5/- ! Those were the days.

Part III

PHOTOFILE

**Remains of Anson T.21 VV955
on the western end of 2,000 feet Tal-y-Fan.**
Terry Thomas via David Roberts

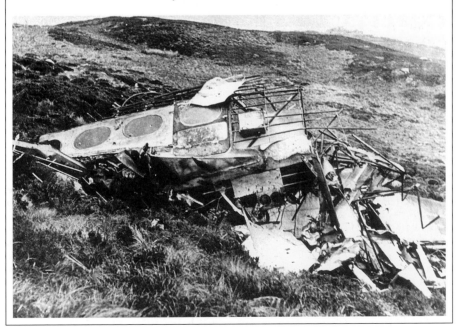

Above: **Avro Anson Mk.XII, similar to the later T.21.** *Harry Holmes*

Anson T.21 VV955

This aircraft, of the Coastal Command Communications Squadron, took off on 20th May 1959 from Bovingdon, Herts, for Ballykelly in Northern Ireland. The pilot was Flight Lieutenant E A Hart, who had survived service in Bomber Command, and navigator Flying Officer F N Handa. Their passenger was Group Captain J E Preston who was to attend an anti-submarine course in Londonderry. Somewhere above the Conway Valley, the crew received orders to divert to RAF Valley, but they never arrived. The writer heard the Anson fly quite low in cloud above Roe Wen, around midday, and was able to advise Valley of this after a news item that evening. The wreckage was spotted by a search Anson the next morning. All on board had been killed instantaneously. Presumably the crew thought they were over the coast near Rhyl with a clear run to Valley when the diversion was made. Some 30 feet higher and the Anson would have cleared the last high ground on the route.

Below, left: **Author's grandchildren Michael, Siân (left) and Laura, being given the 'knowledge', on the ridge where Anson VV955 first hit.** *Author*

Below, right: **Flight Lieutenant Ernest Alfred Hart, known as Nick.** *Mrs Vivien Branscheid*

Remains of Anson T.21 VV955 on the western end of 2,000 feet Tal-y-Fan.
Both Terry Thomas via David Roberts

Beaufighter Mk.I X7845/ Wellington III BK234 Collision

Squadron Leader Roger de Winton Kelsall Winlaw of No.256 Fighter Squadron, was based at RAF Woodvale, near Southport from June 1942, following the move from Squires Gate. On 31st October, Winlaw and his navigator, Pilot Officer C T Ashton, flew to North Wales to take part in a 'Bullseye' exercise in Beaufighter X7845. This involved mock attacks on Wellington bombers, and BK234 became their 'target'. Unfortunately, the two aircraft collided and fell at Perfeddgoed Farm, near Bangor, with the loss of both crews. Squadron Leader Winlaw was cremated a week later and his ashes scattered over the sea. He had been a Master at Harrow School before joining the RAFVR. A son, Roger, was born to his widow, Marsali Mary Winlaw, on 7th February 1943.

Squadron Leader Roger de Winton Kelsall Winlaw. *Roger Winlaw (son)*

Beaufighter TF.X RD210

This aircraft, based at No.1 Ferry Unit, RAF Pershore, was carrying out a fuel consumption test on 10th February 1945 when it disappeared in cloudy conditions. It was later found near the summit of Aran Fawddwy with the bodies of pilot Flying Officer A L Roe, RAAF, and Warrant Officer Newbry.

English Electric Canberra B.2 WK129

On 23rd September 1955, the port undercarriage of this aircraft collapsed on landing at the Radar Research Establishment, Defford. The pilot was Wing Commander Hyland Smith DFC AFC, later Captain of the Queen's Flight. The navigator was Flight Lieutenant Nick Shelley.

Bristol Beaufighter X7543, Mk.VI prototype. *BAe Bristol*

A Bristol Hercules engine from Beaufighter TF.X RD210. *Steve Roberts*

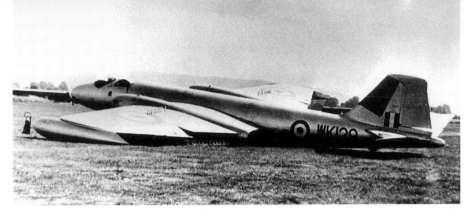

On 9th December 1957 the same aircraft with Shelley's brother, Flight Lieutenant K C F 'Spike' Shelley as navigator, and Flight Lieutenant W A Bell as pilot, flew to North Wales for a trial with the Ministry of Supply radar hut which was situated on the summit of 2,500 feet Drum in the Carneddau. On completion of this the pilot reported on R/T in the vicinity of Puffin Island that he was returning to base. That was his last message. Pershore advised the RAF Valley Mountain Rescue Team that they had an overdue aircraft and a radio appeal for information was

English Electric Canberra B.2 WK129 on 23rd September 1955, after the port undercarriage collapsed. *Glyn Warren*

Flight Lieutenant K C F Shelley. *Glyn Warren*

Engine from the Canberra below the crash site.

broadcast that night. This resulted in two reports. The first was from a young sheep farmer, Oswald Jones, who had been in Cwm Dulyn and heard an explosion about 3.00pm which he took to be an aircraft breaking the sound barrier.

The second came from an electricity board engineer, Mr Adams, in the next cwm who had seen a Canberra flying below cloud. The cloud base was estimated to be at 2,200 feet, with icing at 3,000 feet. The cloud hampered the rescue teams for days, but on the 12th the wreckage of the Canberra and its crew was found close to the summit of Carnedd Llewelyn, the second highest mountain in Wales at 3,484 feet.

The RAF Board of Inquiry could not positively establish the cause of the crash, but considered that engine failure due to icing was the most probable cause. Both airmen are buried at Astwood Cemetery, Worcester, though not in adjacent graves as comrades. Religion dictated otherwise.

Hawker Hunter T.7 XL622

On 17th May 1971 Hawker Hunter XL622 took off from RAF Valley with two experienced flying instructors on board, Flight Lieutenants John Loftus and John Duckworth. They flew to Conwy and proceeded up the valley until turning along the valley of the Afon Machno. At its head the Hunter made a sharp roll to the right but collided with the rock face of Craig Blaen y cwm opposite with the unfortunate loss of both airmen.

Fellow pilots judged the following scenario leading to the crash: The instructors appeared to have set out to practice low speed, bad weather aircraft handling at low level. This could be used in conditions of possibly poor visibility over hostile terrain where the pilot was keeping below radar cover. By flying low and at slow speed there would be a reasonable chance of avoiding any obstacles en route.

The final stage in this case was as the Hunter flew down the narrow valley towards Blaen y cwm at 220 knots and with a little flap to improve handling qualities. In theory as soon as they emerged from the valley they

Above left: Flight Lieutenant John Loftus, with No.8 Sqn at Khormaksar, Aden, in 1967. *Group Captain P Langrill*

Above right: **Flight Lieutenant Timothy Mermagen.** *Toby Mermagen (son)*

Bottom: **A Hunter T.7 from the same unit as XL622 seen at RAF Valley.** *S G Richards*

Photograph on the opposite page:

LAC Tommy W Gurnell, pilot of Oxford N4568. *Jean Langley (sister)*

would turn sharp right and comfortably clear the mountain opposite. There were flaws to this procedure, one on the day. Unknown to the pilots the aircraft was subject to a 40 knot tailwind funnelling down the valley. This would not appear on the airspeed indicator and, as they made the turn, at an unexpected 260 knots, the centrifugal force rapidly took them into Blaen y cwm. As the Hunter was throttled well back, the engine power could not be increased quickly and there was not enough kinetic energy to level out and zoom up over the mountain.

Gnats XR950/XS108 Collision

Flight Lieutenant Timothy Mermagen was an instructor and flight leader of three Gnat T.1s which took off from RAF Valley on 22nd April 1965. He was flying in XR950, with co-pilot Flight Lieutenant Raymond Tyler; the other Gnats in formation had student pilots. One student in XS108 brought his aircraft too close and it collided with XR950. Tyler ejected straight away and only sustained an ankle injury on landing. Flight Lieutenant Mermagen stayed with his aircraft to clear the village of Carmel nearby and lost his life in the ensuing crash. His body was never found. The villagers were convinced his action saved lives and held a collection. Two seats were bought and installed outside the chapel in his memory.

The student pilot in XS108 managed to return to Valley, but lost control on landing, also losing his life.

Oxford Mk.I N4568

Leading Aircraftman Tommy W Gurnell had been in a reserved occupation, but was desperate to fly, so he joined the RAF. On 3rd August 1941, at 11 SFTS Shawbury, he made a rather shaky take-off, just missing the control tower, which agitated him to the effect that he left the local flying area and somehow found his way to the Conway Valley.

Young Ian Deane and his parents were picking bilberries near the head of Sychnant Pass between Conway and Penmaenmawr. He recalls: 'While the cloud was low, it was clear of the local hilltops. Suddenly, as we were sitting there amongst the heather and bilberry shrubs we heard the sound of an

aircraft. It was quite loud and felt lower than it should have been. We looked up and then saw an aeroplane come from behind the hill we were on, heading roughly towards Conway and going downwards. We then heard the sounds of a crash, and soon afterwards saw smoke rising from behind the hill. Father ran off to see if he could do anything, since he thought we were the only people on the hills at the time. He returned to tell us there was nothing that could be done for the pilot, and the police had taken charge. I am quite clear that the plane was not behaving normally. Apart from being too low, and not flying at a reasonable angle, it seemed to be doing a stunt or something risky. I was not surprised when I knew that it had crashed.'

The crash investigation determined that the young pilot had lost control in cloud. This would have resulted in the observation that Ian Deane made.

The crater made by Gloster Meteor F.8
WA794 in Yr Eifl quarry. *MoD*

Part of the tail section of Meteor WA794.
MoD

Meteor F.8 WA794

On 11th October 1957, Sergeant Bob Barnes took off from RAE Llanbedr in Meteor WA794 of No.5 CAACU, to carry out an early morning exercise with the Army at Ty-croes in Anglesey. He had changed places with another pilot so that he could get away that morning for a holiday. At the time, the Yr Eifl range (the Fork Prongs, but commonly known as The Rivals), was covered in a sea mist with a ceiling of 730 feet. Five minutes after take off the pilot reported that he could see through a gap in the mountains. However, he flew to port of the gap and skirted the southern edge of the high ground, appearing to attempt to fly through a narrower gap. In doing so, the Meteor collided with the seaward peak on the topmost quarry face at 1060 feet, with the pilot losing his life. The crash took place at 0700 hours. Just half an hour later and sixty quarrymen would have been working on that level.

On climbing up to the site at that quarry in the sky many years later, to pay my respects, I was guided to the spot by a friendly quarryman. He also tolerantly corrected my knowledge of birdlife. The cliff-dwellers I took to be ravens, he told me, were actually choughs.

Sergeant Bob Barnes, the pilot of the ill-fated Gloster Meteor WA794, seen standing far right of this group, photographed at RAF Duxford. *Mrs M E Barnes.*

A team from RAF Llanbedr search the wreckage of Mosquito TV982 near Snowdon summit. *Ted Cross*

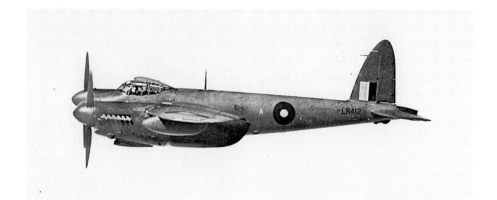

Mosquito FB.VI LR412

This aircraft, from 540 Squadron at Benson, took off on 9th February 1944 for a flap test and then cross-country flight. The Mosquito struck the summit ridge of Aran Fawddwy in cloud at 2,000 feet and the Polish pilot Flying Officer M Ostoja-Slonski and navigator Flying Officer Paul Riches DFC were killed.

Mosquito T.III TV982

This aircraft took off from Horsham St.Faith, near Norwich on 31st July 1948 to fly to Alder-grove, near Belfast, after a Royal Auxiliary Air Force summer camp. The pilot gave a lift to Corporal Carlisle who was anxious to see twins just born to his wife. Unfortunately, the Mosquito flew into cumulo-nimbus thunder cloud and broke up, falling near the summit of Snowdon, with no chance for the pilot or passenger to bale out.

Vampire FB.5 VV601

This aircraft took off with pilot Midshipman R M Armitage RNVR on a solo aerobatic exercise over northern Snowdonia. It later dived into the side of the mountain above Hafod y Rhiw near Llyn Eigiau, at an angle of 20 degrees, with wings level, killing the pilot. The cause of the accident was obscure, but the aircraft appeared to be out of control. However, a mild steel bar, not part of the Vampire, was discovered in the cockpit in a

Top: **Mosquito FB.VI LR412.** *IWM*

Centre left: **Midshipman R M Armitage, RNVR.** *Derby Evening Telegraph via R G Patilla.*

Centre right: **Sergeant Frederick W Maskell, pilot of Wellington LB185.** *Jimmy Jarman*

Bottom: **Mosquito T.III LR412 memorial at the gate of Esgair-gawr, near Rhydymain on the A494.**

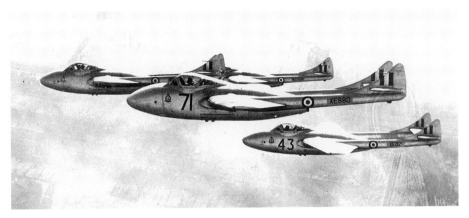

minute search of the wreckage taken away. This may well have jammed the elevator controls.

Wellington Mk.VIII LB185
Sergeant Frederick W Maskell was rear gunner on Wellington LB185 flying from 6 OTU at Haverfordwest on 20th November 1943.

A flight of Vampire T.11s from 4 FTS at RAF Valley. *R E (Bob) Roberts*

Crater carved by de Havilland Vampire FB.5 VV601 on 19th April 1956, now carpeted with pink heather.

Lost, and running short of fuel the pilot elected to reduce height through cloud for a fix, only to collide with Moel y Croesau, near Trawsfynydd. Sergeants Maskell and A Sinclair were the only survivors, with an injured Sinclair going off for help through the night. Maskell was rammed into a bog, and was extracted with great difficulty since he had spinal and other injuries.

Sergeant Maskell spent the rest of his life in various hospitals, and went to the Star and Garter Home in Richmond in November 1945. He died there, as a result of his wartime injuries, on 21st January 1946.

No.34 Maintenance Unit, RAF Detachment at Bethesda

The main centre for recovery of crashed and forced-landed aircraft in North Wales and the borders was No.34 Maintenance Unit at Monkmoor, Shrewsbury. Snowdonia (as with other mountain areas in the U.K.) became such a hazard to aircraft movements that a detachment was set up in a central position, at the football ground in Bethesda, the only reasonably level piece of ground in that locality.

In April 1943 Dick Morris was posted there from Monkmoor as a member of the salvage team under the command of Flying Officer Parry. All the lads were billeted on local people, Dick at No.26 Adwyr Nant with Mr & Mrs Buckland. 'Our main gathering place at night was the 'Bull' public house run by Wilf and Mary Bullock, ably assisted by Mrs Price Morris who lived across the road. Once a week we had pictures at the village hall. The picture had to be good to distract us from the hard wooden seats. We got on well with the local populace. They opened the tennis club in winter. A radiogram was obtained and dances were organised. A trip to Bangor to the pictures meant that you had to catch the last bus, run by Purple Motors, at 9.30 pm. To see the end of a film we often did our share of the long walk back.

'Our HQ was made from two large packing cases, which had contained Hurricane fighters, tacked onto the soccer pavilion. The field itself was divided up into areas for each main type of aircraft brought in. Where unusable wreckage had to be destroyed, petrol was poured over and set alight with a Verey pistol. All went well until one day when an oleo leg exploded and a piece of it headed like a rocket and hit one of our two Polish members, Sergeant Sikowski, on the leg. A leg for a leg. None were burnt after that'.

Dick Morris was an armourer, but he and Fred Puddifer became experts at removing engines. From the numbers of engines still on high ground in the 1970s, these must have been fairly low ground incidents. In fact this was not an assortment of general duties ground crew, but a team of skilled technicians, armourers, airframe and engine mechanics. The MT drivers included the driver of a large Coles crane, and the movement of this vehicle caused many problems. Dick Morris: 'The gate in the town walls near Conway Castle, and the start of the B5106 was OK for the big square-nosed Bedford, but the Coles crane got stuck in the roof of the gate. We had to go back and make a long detour. Strangely, it would get through going downhill. Another time we collected an Oxford that had come down at Tyn-y-Groes (W6628 on 24.07.43.), placed it on a 60 feet Queen Mary transporter, and headed for Bethesda via Llanrwst. Here we could not get past a Belisha Beacon just on the bad bend towards the town square. We fitted a rope to the top of it and, with the assistance of the market day crowd, pulled it over to pass. Unfortunately, we then got an engine bearer stuck fast on a shop blind no-one had noticed. It didn't look so good when we finally got past.

'Of the many crashes in the hills we attended, I recall the ingenuity we came up with for the Anson crash above Cowlyd (LT433 on 20.02.44.) After looking at the crash we went back to Bethesda where we went to the local garage, where we obtained two bumpers from old cars. In those days they were made to stand up to their name. We made a timber platform, and fitted the detachable bumpers, so it could be carried up the mountains in sections and assembled there. We fitted tow ropes and brought most of the Anson down over a week. It was one of our classics.

'We also helped the RAF Llandwrog Mountain Rescue Teams when they were searching for missing aircraft. The Humber ambulance was the control base at the foot of the mountains. It had an Aldis lamp on the roof so that we could find our way back, and had a tent fitted at the back to shelter from the often severe weather. One policeman from Bethesda used to come out with us and wait for our return in the Humber's tent. He is the only man I have ever seen who could sleep standing up – it was so warm in there when you came in from the cold'.

Les Mellor's most vivid recollection is attending the USAAF C-47 Skytrain (Dakota) crash in the Carneddau: 'It was on a dangerous rocky ledge high above Dulyn Lake. The Mountain Rescue team had gone to it via Tal-y-Bont, but we went over the mountains from Bethesda via Gerlan and dropped down to it from the tops. Most of the front section and wings had been destroyed, What was left of the fuselage and tailplane was hanging out from the ledge over the lake. We assisted the Medical Officer and rescue chaps to recover the four bodies of the crew. It was so bitterly cold and wet and we had many weary miles to go to reach civilisation. As soon as we reached our transport waiting in Tal-y-Bont, Flying Officer Parry treated us all royally to a tot of whisky in the pub there'.

The many parts recovered were either placed in the spares system where crashes were not severe, or scrap aluminium was ultimately melted down for various functions of the war effort, including new aircraft. Ansons, with wooden wings were burned after useable parts were salvaged.

Also, the sites had to be reasonably cleared so that they would not be reported as newly crashed aircraft by pilots overflying. The Douglas Boston on Carnedd Dafydd was reported several times after the original crash in October 1942, causing the Llandwrog Mountain Rescue Team to be called out unnecessarily; the lads were not pleased.

34 MU team salvage Anson Mk.I LT433 parts above Llyn Cowlyd. The odd recovered flying helmet was put to good use. *Dick Morris*

Members of 34 MU detachment at Bethesda. Back row L-R, unknown, Percy Stenning, Bob Goss, Noel –. Middle row, unknown, Eddie Holden, Ginger Taylor, Robbie Robinson. Front Row, Les Mellor, Mich –, Sylvia –, Wyn Foster, George Starr, Sgt King. *Dick Morris*

Stripping down a Hurricane at 34 MU, Bethesda. *David Roberts*

Appendix B

Royal Observer Corps at Caernarvon Castle

Before the Second World War, little thought was given by the Air Ministry to any Luftwaffe attack on north-west Britain. It was assumed that France would hold firm in any war, and possible air attacks would come directly from Germany. However, Hitler was no gentleman and his troops simply by-passed the Maginot line taking almost everyone by surprise. Fortunately the main architect of air defence, Air Chief Marshal Sir Hugh Dowding, had organised a committee to look into an overall air defence scheme to include Observer Corps reports being filtered into air raid warnings, and to Fighter Command. In March 1939 No.26 Group Observer Corps HQ was set up at Wrexham telephone exchange, and posts came into being in increasing numbers across north-east Wales.

However, it was not until October 1940, as the Battle of Britain came to a conclusion, that Caernarvon Castle became the HQ of the Corps for No.28/2 Group covering north-west Wales. This nerve centre was situated in the Eagle Tower, with administration and operations room, collating and plotting reports. The HQ was under the command of Captain J W Sanders, with Mr C C Vallance as Controller. Observers could climb to the giddy heights at the top of the Eagle Tower to view Llandwrog Ansons as the pilots waved to their girl friends below. A network of posts in Anglesey and the mainland passed reports of aircraft movements to the centre. The new Corps organisation was only just in time for the night Blitz in the winter of 1940/41. This included Luftwaffe bombers flying up the west coast of Wales to attack targets on Merseyside and the north-west from recently captured French airfields. RAF Valley in Anglesey would be opened in February 1941,

and other fighter stations in the north-west were already on hand to do the raiders harm. The input of reports from the Observer Corps, which was awarded the prefix Royal after the Battle of Britain, was invaluable.

The ROC had other facets. Observers tracked our own and allied aircraft and, should any not arrive at their destination, a last course and position was available to searchers. In the mountain areas, posts could light the 'Granite' system, red signal flares in the form of squares, should aircraft be in danger by low flying in cloud or at night. This was along with 'Darky', a radio system operated at remote posts to give aircraft in distress a course to steer to the nearest airfield. By the end of hostilities it was estimated that around 7,000 aircraft were saved with ROC help, a huge saving in lives.

One observer who served at Caernarvon Castle was so taken with their vital role that she was later inspired to write a poem;

To all the Gallant Lads

A castle at Caernarvon our home was to be,
For we were members of the R.O.C.,
Plotting aircraft from the Eagle Tower,
Day and night long, hour by hour.

A worthwhile job this turned out to be,
Information flowing from this fortress by the sea,
Guiding our lads on missions they made,
Hoping our loved ones would never fade.

We plotted their journeys on the 'ops' table there,
While they were careering through the air.
Doing their bit for all of us here,
As we were waiting for the sound 'All Clear'.

Evelyn Goldsmith (née Hall-Williams).

A bevy of ROC beauties at Caernarvon Castle. L-R Back Row, 3rd Miss Morris, 7th Frances Jones, 8th Mrs Williams, 10th Eirwen Hughes. Middle Row, 1st Ella Jones, 2nd Una Roberts, 4th Sheila Rathbone Owen, 5th Miss Ellis, 6th Mary Davies, 7th Ruby Winch. Front Row, 1st Mrs Hill, 3rd Miss Evelyn Hall Williams, 5th Minnie Jones.
Ruby Bishop

Royal Observer Corps members in the grounds of Caernarvon Castle. L-R Back row, 4th Minnie Jones, 5th Mr Green, 6th Mr C C Vallance, Controller, 7th Mr Jones, 10th Frances Jones, 14th Mr Angel, 17th Mrs Williams. Middle Row, 2nd Ruby Winch, 3rd Miss Morris, 4th Ella Jones, 6th Sheila Rathbone Owen, 7th Miss Ellis. Front Row, 2nd Mary Davies, 4th Eve Hall Williams, 7th Miss Williams, 8th Glenys Williams.
Ruby Bishop

The ROC operations room at Caernarvon Castle. The Ansons from Llandwrog, Penrhos, and later Mona, would always be a major feature on the plotting table.
Ruby Bishop

British Military Aircraft Crashes in Snowdonia since 1960

The majority of the military post-war crashes in Snowdonia are from No.4 Flying Training School at RAF Valley, where the de Havilland Vampires of the 1950s gave way to the Folland Gnat in the 1960s and 1970s along with some Hawker Hunters from 1967, then to the BAe Hawk from 1980 to the present day.

FOLLAND GNAT T.1

27.05.64	XR949	4FTS	Crew ejected OK, after hood fractured, aircraft flew into Arenig Fawr
22.07.64	XR978	4FTS	Abandoned in inverted spin, aircraft crashed into drained Llyn Celyn reservoir, narrowly missing workmen. Pilot OK, but instructor found badly injured on nearby Mynydd Nodol.
22.04.65	XR950	4FTS	Collision over Carmel. 1 killed, 1 ejected OK.
	XS108	4FTS	Collision over Carmel. 1 killed on landing.
13.05.66	XR539	4FTS	Abandoned in spin, crew ejected OK. Aircraft fell on or near Y Cnicht.
23.05.66	XR570	4FTS	Hit HT cables nr Llyn Celyn. Pilot ejected OK. *
13.06.69	XR952	4FTS	Loss of control in spin nr A5 at Glasfryn, pilot ejected OK.
14.03.72	XR948	4FTS	Engine failure 3m NE Llanbedr, pilot ejected OK.
16.10.75	XS106	4FTS	Loss of control in spin, crashed 1m N Llanrwst, pilot ejected OK.
30.04.76	XP536	4FTS	Low level collision in which both pupil pilots.
	XR983	4FTS	and their instructors were killed. The Gnats fell on high ground at Llety Canol farm near Brithdir, two miles from Dolgelly.

BAe HAWK T.1

14.06.89	XX182	4FTS	Collision over Borth. Pilot ejected OK.
	XX291	4FTS	Collision over Borth. 1 killed.

HAWKER HUNTER T.7

17.05.71	XL622	4FTS	Flew into high ground at Craig Blaen y Cwm, near. Cwm Penmachno, 2 killed.

WESTLAND GAZELLE HT.3

20.04.83	XX374	2FTS	Crashed on Snowdon while low-flying, 2 killed.

WESTLAND WESSEX HC.2

12.08.93	XR524	22 Sqn	Crashed into Llyn Padarn on training flight. 3 ATC cadets killed, 3 crew and 1 cadet survived.

* Pilot, P/O Terence Jones, saw a mystery object while low flying, and ejected as he could not see ahead. Two anglers saw a shining object fall into the lake. It was not a seagull, they said.

Precision shot of Folland Gnat T.1 XP503 circling Caernarfon Castle. *Bob Roberts*

'Shep' investigates an intruder on his patch – Gnat T.1 XR949 tail section on Arenig Fawr. *Bob Roberts*

Gnat T.1 XR949 prepares for take off at RAF Valley. *Bob Roberts*

Gnat T.1 XS106 cockpit canopy at the door of Pen y Bryn, near Llanrwst. *Glyn Davies*

Bibliography, Museums and Memorials

BIBLIOGRAPHY

Charlwood, Don: *No Moon Tonight*;
Goodall Publications, 1984.

Charlwood, Don: *Journeys into Night*;
Hudson, 1991.

Doylerush, Edward: *No Landing Place*;
Midland Counties Publications, 1985.

Doylerush, Edward: *Fallen Eagles*;
Midland Counties Publications, 1990.

Doylerush, Edward: *The Legend of Lland-wrog*; Midland Counties Publications, 1994.

Hastings, Max: *Bomber Command*;
Pan Books, 1981.

Hill, Terence R: *Down in Wales*;
Gwasg Carreg Gwlach, 1994.

Hill, Terence R: *Down in Wales 2*;
Gwasg Carreg Gwalch, 1996.

Jones, Ivor Wynne: *Attack from the West*;
Liverpool Daily Post articles,
14-17th November 1966.

Kilford, Major C R: *Lethbridge at War*;
Battery Books & Publications, 1996.
Includes story of PoW camps at Medicine Hat, Canada.

Oliver, David: *British Military Aircraft Accidents, The Last 25 Years;* Ian Allan, 1990.

Poucher, W A: *The Welsh Peaks;*
Constable. Splendid photography and detailed routes to all the main peaks.

Sloan, Roy: *Wings of War over Gwynedd*;
Gwasg Carreg Gwlach, 1991.

Sloan, Roy: *Aircraft Crashes, Flying Accidents in Gwynedd 1910-1990;*
Gwasg Carreg Gwlach, 1994.

Smith, David J: *High Ground Wrecks 3rd edn*;
Midland Counties Publications, 1989.

Smith, David J: *High Ground Wrecks & Relics 4th edn*; Midland Counties Pubs, 1997.

Smith, David J: *Britain's Military Airfields 1939-45*; Patrick Stephens Ltd, 1989.

MUSEUMS

Caernarfon Air World, Caernarfon Airport.
Aircraft, exhibits, many photographs, including an RAF Mountain Rescue section.

RAF Cosford, nr Wolverhampton. Many historic aircraft including Dakota, Liberator, and Mosquito.

Fort Perch Rock, New Brighton. Excellent display of recovered aircraft parts, includes C-47 tail fin from Llyn Dulyn & other pieces from Snowdonia.

Maes Artro Village, nr Harlech. Museum includes Anson restoration and Jindivik at old RAF Llanbedr living quarters.

AVIATION MEMORIALS

Plaque at Pennal War Memorial:
Wellington R1068, 17.08.41.

Plaque on summit of Arenig Fawr, and on Old Town Hall, Bala:
B-17 Fortress 42-3124, 04.08.43.

Plaque on crash site at Moelfre, above Llanfairfechan:
B-24 Liberator 42-99991, 07.01.44.

Plaque on engine at Drws-y-Coed:
Mosquito LR412, 09.02.44.

Plaque at lay-by in Llanberis Pass:
B-26 Marauder 44-68072, 01.02.45.

Plaque at crash site on Rhinog Fawr:
Lancaster NE132, 06.02.45.

Plaque near crash site on Craig Cwm Llwyd: B-17 Fortress 44-8639, 08.06.45.

Bilingual plaques on Llyn Padarn shore, Llanberis, for 3 ATC cadets: Wessex XR524, 12.08.93.

One young local man, Robert Jones, was so moved by the Snowdonia losses that he has placed a small slate memorial at many of the sites. (see bottom photo on p.112 overleaf)

Two Memorial plaques (in Welsh and English) to three ATC cadets on the shore of Llyn Padarn, opposite Piggery Pottery.

Memorial plaque at Pennal War Memorial to the crew of Wellington R1068.

Memorial in Cwm Edno to those killed on board the Aer Lingus Dakota on 10th January 1952. *Ian Cooper*

Robert Jones visits crash sites with a slate plaque, like this one for the crew of Wellington DV800 on Ysgolion Duon (Black Ladders).

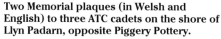

Maps

The Ordnance Survey 1:50000 series will be useful to follow this book. Sheets 115 and 124 cover the main area with sheets 123 and 125 if required. Crash locations are detailed in the original *No Landing Place,* which is still in print in 1999, available from many outlets in the Snowdonia area, or in case of difficulty, direct from the publishers, price £6.95.

Aircraft Wreckage

The remains of crashed British, German and United States military aircraft are the responsibility of the Ministry of Defence. Recovery operations may not be carried out without the permission of the MoD.

Contact point for recovery groups is: MoD Air Force Board Secretariat, Room 8239, Main Building, Whitehall, London, SW1A 2HB.

Snowdonia National Park

The Park is not open range country. The land all belongs to someone – mainly farmers and The National Trust.

Permission from the MoD to recover wreckage must be followed by an agreement with an individual landowner to dig at a site. The normal requirements of the Country Code should be observed and indicated public footpaths adhered to.